DESERT SANCTUARIES

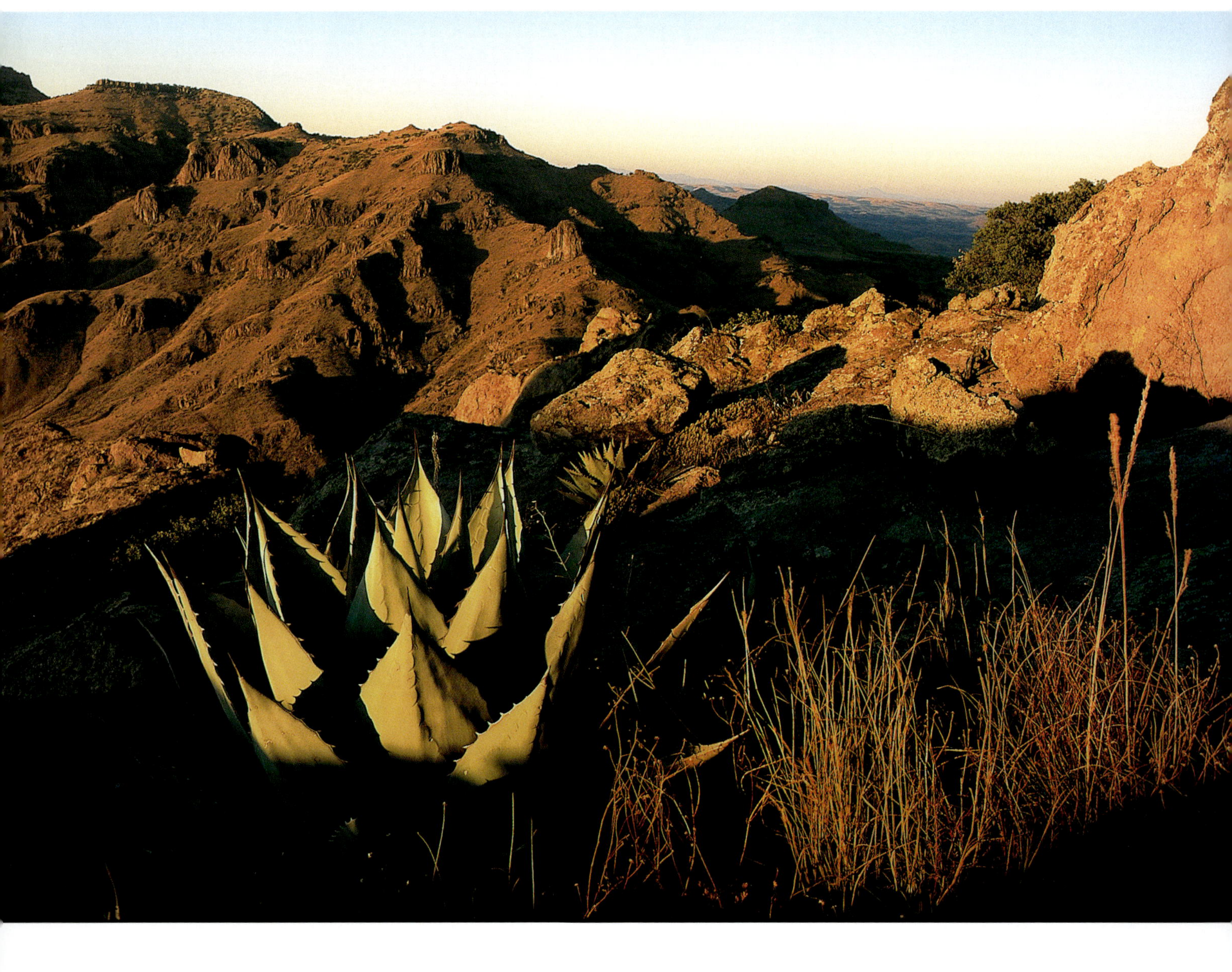

desert sanctuaries

The Chinatis of the Big Bend

WYMAN MEINZER

Introduction by David Alloway

TEXAS TECH UNIVERSITY PRESS

This book is typeset in Monotype Dante. The paper used in this book meets the minimum requirements of ANSI/NISO Z39.48-1992 (R1997). ∞

Designed by Barbara Werden
Frontispiece: Eastern rim, San Antonio Canyon

Printed in China at Everbest Printing Company

02 03 04 05 06 07 08 09 10 / 9 8 7 6 5 4 3 2 1

Texas Tech University Press
Box 41037
Lubbock, Texas 79409-1037 USA
1.800.832.4042
ttup@ttu.edu
www.ttup.ttu.edu

Library of Congress Cataloging-in-Publication Data

Meinzer, Wyman.
Desert sanctuaries : the Chinatis of the Big Bend / photographs by Wyman Meinzer ; introduction by David Alloway.
p. cm.
ISBN 0-89672-488-3 (cloth : alk. paper) — ISBN 0-89672-489-1 (pbk. : alk. paper)
1. Big Bend Region (Tex.) — Pictorial works. 2. Chinati Mountains (Tex.) — Pictorial works. I. Title.

F392.B54 B43 2002
976.4'93 — dc21

2002007379

To my loving wife

SYLINDA HUNTER-MEINZER

who continues to support my insatiable appetite for adventure, and to those people of the desert who live and thrive in some of the harshest conditions on earth.

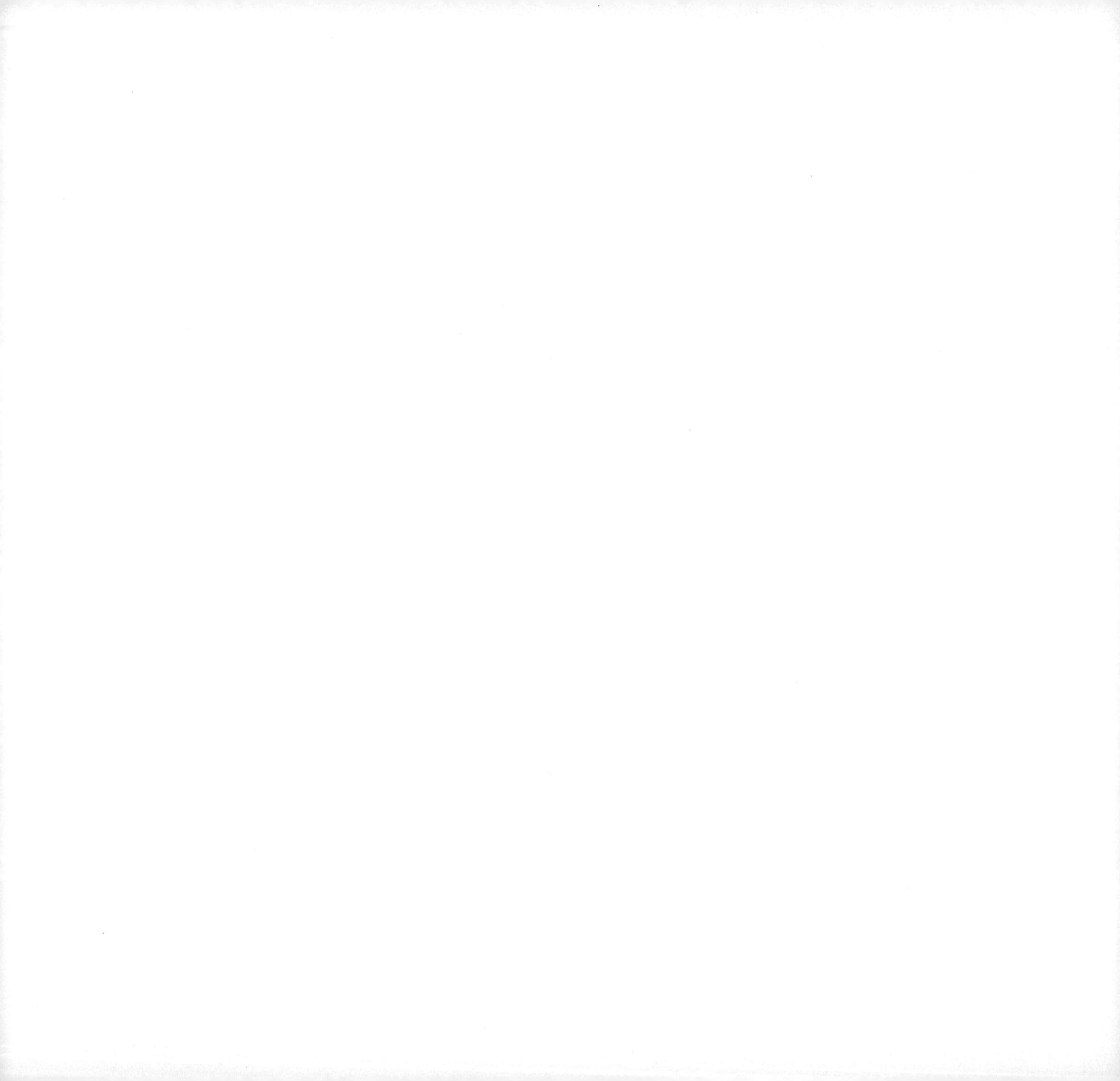

ACKNOWLEDGMENTS

My first introduction to the Big Bend region of Texas was some fourteen years ago when my friend Knut Mjolhus and I flew several hours in a Cessna 206 over the Big Bend Ranch shooting aerial photographs for *Texas Parks and Wildlife* magazine. Knut and I, plainsmen from Amarillo and Benjamin respectively, were intrigued by the formidable topography and relative isolation of this Chihuahuan desert region and were soon planning a future photographic endeavor into some of the more remote areas of the Big Bend. Upon our arrival back to the wide expanses of the Panhandle and Rolling Plains, the memories of our trip were not diminished. Thus we vowed to return someday to record on film some of the hidden sanctuaries of this desert stronghold in far West Texas. Like the explorers of early day Texas, when knowledgeable guides were essential in the success of expeditions into unfamiliar lands, we could not have secured the images in these pages without the approval and involvement of many wonderful people from within and outside this spectacular region, famous for its beautiful and forbidding scenery.

To describe each one's involvement would take volumes, so I will just mention names. I am deeply indebted to the Texas Parks and Wildlife Department, and to my dear friends Andrew Sansom, Walt Dabney, and Delton Daugherty for understanding the importance of recording the pristine condition of these locations for the wonderment of future generations; also to Luis Armendariz and Al Real, two patriarchs of the desert who also appreciated my goal of recording these Chihuahuan treasures. My first introduction to the Chinatis was in the fine company of Jim Carrico, a Lajitas resident and former Superintendent of the Big Bend National Park who shares my sentiments regarding the sanctuaries shown herein. And my sincere appreciation to David Alloway, a two-legged desert fox, who understands the fragility of life in this formidable region and so kindly agreed to share his vast knowledge of the Big Bend Ranch State Park and Chinati Mountains State Natural Area in writing the enlightening introduction within these pages.

Of course, I can never say enough regarding the contribution of my friend and pilot Knut Mjolhus for sharing my love of adventure and selflessly offering his aircraft to gain access to some of the most hostile landscape in the state of Texas. Without his expert piloting and navigational skills, most of the images contained in this book would not have been possible.

INTRODUCTION

I am a privileged person. Since 1975, I have lived, studied, worked, and played in the Big Bend region of Texas. In 1988, the Texas Parks and Wildlife Department purchased the Big Bend Ranch. The new addition to Texas Parks and Wildlife fully doubled the acreage of the state parks system in Texas, and I represented the Big Bend Archeological Society at public meetings in support of the acquisition. I also served as head of education at Big Bend Ranch State Park for ten years. During that time, additional land purchases and donations added to the park's already considerable size. The most notable donations were those from the Rice and Diekert families — 11,000 acres on the northern boundary and over 4,000 acres on the park's eastern edge respectively. These donations pushed the holdings to over 470 square miles. In 1996, the Mellon Foundation donated the Mesquite Ranch to Texas Parks and Wildlife. The new property fell under the stewardship of the administrative office at Big Bend Ranch State Park, and another of my privileges was to help in the initial planning for this important and generous gift, which later became Chinati Mountains State Natural Area.

This book explores Big Bend Ranch State Park and Chinati Mountains State Natural Area. Through the photography of Wyman Meinzer, we are able to view the remote corners of the land that few are fortunate enough to intimately explore.

In 1997, by declaration of the Seventy-fifth Legislature and with the approval of Governor George W. Bush, Wyman Meinzer was named the State Photographer of Texas. For his friends and patrons, this was merely confirmation of what we had known for years. I have been fortunate enough to spend much time with Wyman, and it is clear that he has the technical knowledge of a photographer, the eye of an artist, the heart of an explorer, and the pride of a Texan. Wyman has dedicated his life to capturing the wondrous variety of Texas landscapes and history with his camera. He and his close friend and pilot Knut Mjolhus roam the state by foot, four-wheel drive, and helicopter in search of the places few will ever know. Wyman tackles the most rugged terrain with burdens of photographic gear, but stops at nothing to get the photograph he wants — the photograph that captures the land at its best.

When broken down into technical terms, photography is simply the transfer of reflected light onto a chemical film that undergoes a change in color or contrast. Quality photography requires knowledge of light, exposure times, aperture settings, film speeds, and processing; however, one cannot achieve the emotion contained in a Wyman Meinzer photograph with merely an expensive camera and technical know-how. Placing a border around the vastness of Big Bend is typically an invitation to disappointment. Reducing its depth to a medium of two dimensions tends to flatten a landscape known to be anything but flat. Catching the ever-changing moods of light and color in fractions of a second normally embalms the scene. So how does Wyman give us photos full of expansive depth and color? His skill is his passion for the beauty of Texas and his unwavering will to get to the toughest spots. He is an adventurer first and a photographer second. Wyman *feels* the land and sky. He becomes a part of the terrain, and his photos make you part of the scenery.

Big Bend Ranch State Park and Chinati Mountains State Natural Area are among the roughest places I have ever visited. Their origins lie in some of the most dramatic volcanic eruptions known in geological history. From twenty-eight to forty-two million years ago, up to 300 cubic kilometers of material was ejected in what is now Big Bend Ranch and over 1,000 cubic kilometers in the Chinati Mountains region. For comparison's sake, Mt. Saint Helens ejected only *one* kilometer in its famous eruption of 1980. Resulting from the quick cooling lava and ash flow, the landscape today is strewn with loose rock that makes off-trail travel challenging and, at times, dangerous. The rough terrain of the Big Bend area weeds out the sissies and supplies the perfect habitat for people like Wyman Meinzer. The only terrain I have encountered that is more difficult to cross is El Malpais in New Mexico. Its young lava beds have not been rounded by erosion and can cut the soles off new boots in one good hike.

Massive earthquakes twenty-four million years ago added to the Big Bend's ruggedness. During the basin and range faulting, the entire American Southwest was stretched by blocks of land sinking and rising to create the signature mesas and plateaus of the region. Erosion completed the carving of the landscape as the Rio Grande cut deep canyons through the mountains and mesas in a short (geologically speaking) two million years. Tributaries to the ancestral Rio Grande formed the long and yawning Tapado, Madera, Rancherías, and Fresno Canyons on the Big Bend Ranch. The narrow slot of Closed Canyon may not compare in length and depth with other gorges in the region, but the fact that it can, in places, be spanned with outstretched arms makes it a rare place for hiking in the shade.

Perhaps the most fascinating geological feature on the Big Bend Ranch is the gaping cavity Solitario. Translated from Spanish as "hermit", the name offers a fitting description for this remote and lonely place. With an outside diameter of up to nine miles, it can be identified from space. The feature began as a *laccolith* — a bulge pushed up in the Earth's crust by pressure of magma. Typically, the magma cools, leaving a dome with a solid core. Solitario, however, could not contain the pressure and erupted approximately thirty-five million years ago. The explosion is believed to have killed every life form within fifty miles. With the pressure expended, the volcano collapsed, forming what geologists call a *caldera*, which takes its name from the Spanish word for caldron. The overlying rock, formed mostly by ancient seas, tilted skyward into concentric rings of mountains and ridges, giving the appearance of a bull's-eye target from high altitudes. The discovery of the origins of Solitario prompted a new geological term, *lacco-caldera*. Solitario is one of only four known in the entire world.

In wetter times, Solitario contained a great deal of water that dissolved the caverns into slanted layers of limestone. During the periods of violent earthquakes, the cavern roofs collapsed, forming the three main canyons that drain the Solitario. These are known as the Shutups. The longest is the Lower Shutup at Solitario's southern edge. Walking the canyon bottom through the rim of Solitario to the keeps of Fresno Canyon, one passes eroded stalactites hanging from the walls, fossil shellfish pavements, and side pockets lined with convoluted layers of two-feet-thick banded calcite, which resemble ribbon candy on a large scale.

The Lower Shutup is my favorite hike, but typically for any hike in the area, not an easy one. In July of 1998, I walked out of it with three men who were training for a 700-mile camel trek in the Empty Quarter of Arabia. Our electronic thermometer read 118 degrees Fahrenheit just before it quit working, bringing true relevance to the word "caldera."

The high temperatures of the area are to be expected as Big Bend Ranch State Park and Chinati Mountains State Natural Area are both located in the northern Chihuahuan Desert. By some definitions, the Chihua-huan is the largest of the North American deserts and has the most diverse flora and fauna. More species of birds are seen each year in Big Bend National Park than in any other National Park in the United States, and the count at Big Bend Ranch State Park is expected to equal or surpass it. Plant species collected at Big Bend Ranch State Park currently number over 1,100 and are predicted to exceed 2,000. Although no natural surveys have been completed at the time of this writing, it is likely that Chinati Mountains State Natural Area produces an even larger number of plant species since the Chinati Mountains rise more than 2,000 feet above those found on the Big Bend Ranch.

Those species that are found in both areas sometimes show a marked dimorphism. For example, the mature lechuguilla and ocotillo of Chinati Mountains State Natural Area are easily one third larger than the same species at Big Bend Ranch State Park. But since Chinati Mountains State Natural Area is relatively new and little research has been completed, the reasons for this type of variance are not yet understood.

The flora and fauna of the Big Bend region can be confusing for first-time visitors. The agave plant sends up a huge bloom stalk that, in its early stages, resembles a giant asparagus spear. The ocotillo is often mistaken for a cactus, even though it is from an entirely separate family with only eleven other species to share its taxonomical niche. Because of their wicked two-inch spines, mounds of low-growing cactus, pitayas, quickly convert the newcomer to an admirer of their large pink blossoms followed by a fruit that tastes amazingly similar to strawberries. The cactus daiquiri is a delicacy little known outside of the region. Even the Hinckley Oak, which holds dubious recognition as an endangered species, finds habitat on the Big Bend Ranch.

Mountain lions and their bobcat cousins roam the countryside, but are rarely visible. Ocelots have been spotted in the area — two fleeting and unconfirmed sightings occurred on the Big Bend Ranch in the mid 1990s. Javelinas, which are commonly found in jungles but have adapted to and flourish in the rugged Big Bend, are often mistaken by newcomers for pigs. The coatimundi, a large relative of the raccoon, and its smaller kin, the ringtail, are also local inhabitants. The ringtail, which looks like a hybrid between a raccoon and a house cat, is one of the more common animals, but its strictly nocturnal hunting habits make it a rare sight for visitors.

On occasion, travelers barge into park visitor centers with breathless reports of bright pink snakes stretched across the highway. The red racer, a variety of the normally black coachwhip, is often sighted due to its daylight hunting practice and pink or red scales that act as anything *but* camouflage. The area also hosts more bat species than any similar-sized area in the United States. Several species have been identified, including the diminutive Western Pipistrelle, the smallest bat in the U.S., and the Western Mastiff, the largest.

Just as the flora and fauna of the region illustrate the diverse nature of the land, so do its former people. Archeological sites abound with the ancient hearths of hunter-gatherers and cryptic rock art of cultures long vanished. The first recorded European and African entry into the region was that of the castaways Cabeza de Vaca, Dorantes, Castillo, and the black Moor Esteban in 1535. Traders from the Aztec empire brought their wares north, and a ball made of local *guayule* rubber was found at an archeological site in Arizona. Patarabueye Indians farmed the Rio Grande flood plains at the time of Spanish exploration and traded crops for dried meat and hides with the Jumanos, who hunted bison on foot. Later the Apache and Comanche would use the region as a place to mount raids into Mexico.

The Spanish kept a tenuous grip on the region, which was divided between the provinces of Tejas y Coahuila and Nueva Viscaya. Dedicated priests ventured into Big Bend in 1683 to build their missions, but military protection was not available until small adobe garrisons were built in the vast desert expanses some ninety years later. José Rodriquez, a bandit in the early 1600s, buried vast fortunes of silver in the desert — treasures not yet found. His alias, "Chinate," means blackbird and gave the Chinati Mountains their name.

Benjamin Leaton became one of the first Anglo settlers in the region, establishing a trading post at Presidio in 1848. The massive adobe structure now stands as the western entrance station for Big Bend Ranch State Park. The region also hosted the familiar Old West cast of soldiers, cowboys, outlaws, miners, and trappers, along with a few visitors who might have seemed out of place. West of Presidio on Highway FM 170 stand the unmarked graves of thirteen Frenchmen, possibly sent by Emperor Maximilian, who ruled Mexico in the 1860s. Their tour of Big Bend ended at the hands of resident Apaches.

The twentieth century also provided its share of notable citizens. Chinese farmers grew rice in the extreme southeast portion of Big Bend Ranch at Lajitas in the early 1900s. Hallie Stillwell, the Grand Dame of Big Bend, taught school in Presidio with a loaded pistol in her desk as the Mexican Revolution raged on the opposite side of the border. Her family ranched in the upper reaches of Fresno Canyon. Ross Maxwell, a pioneer geologist of the region, later became the first Superintendent of Big Bend National Park. Dr. Barton Warnock, a locally-raised botanist and professor at Sul Ross State University, gained legendary status for his research, which began in the 1930s, on Big Bend flora. The Barton Warnock Environmental Education Center at Lajitas is now the eastern entrance station to Big Bend Ranch State Park.

Two men who did not live in Big Bend but recognized its need to be preserved are Bob Armstrong and Andrew Sansom. As Land Commissioner of the State of Texas and later as a Commissioner with Texas Parks and Wildlife Department, Bob Armstrong battled and negotiated with the Texas Legislature for thirteen years to acquire the Big Bend Ranch. His dream was fully realized in 1988 with the purchase of 216,000 acres, which has grown to over

301,000 acres through additional acquisitions. Bob Armstrong will be remembered as the Father of Big Bend Ranch State Park. While Executive Director of the Nature Conservancy of Texas, Andy Sansom also championed the cause of acquiring the huge ranch. Soon after the acquisition, he was appointed as Executive Director of Texas Parks and Wildlife Department, a position to which he brought honor for eleven years.

In the midst of these developments, I was privileged to be responsible for interpreting the incredible natural and cultural resources of these two great places. I felt as if I walked among giants, and I am not alone in that emotion.

While all of these wonders converge to make Big Bend Ranch State Park and Chinati Mountains State Natural Area among the most precious possessions of Texas, many people visit simply to be a part of what Texas was in its raw and wild infancy. The attraction is the remote setting, the tranquillity and silence, and the landscape that seems forbidding while inviting. These places bring out a primal spirit of adventure that is increasingly needed as wild land is tamed and falls before the bulldozer. These are places where people meet challenges and earn their freedom.

And as if I have not been blessed enough, I am privileged once again. One spring day as I bounced along two rock-strewn ruts identified as a road leading to Mexicano and Madrid Falls, Wyman asked if I would write the introduction for this book. This volume is not merely a collection of pretty pictures. It is the result of weeks and miles of rough roads and tough hikes to share the gifts of Wyman Meinzer's vision. It is the documentation of the labors of many who sought to keep Big Bend Ranch State Park and Chinati Mountains State Natural Area a refuge for the future. These are photographs of the spirit of Texas.

DAVID ALLOWAY

OVERLEAF: Agave grassland ridge between San Antonio and Pelillos Canyons

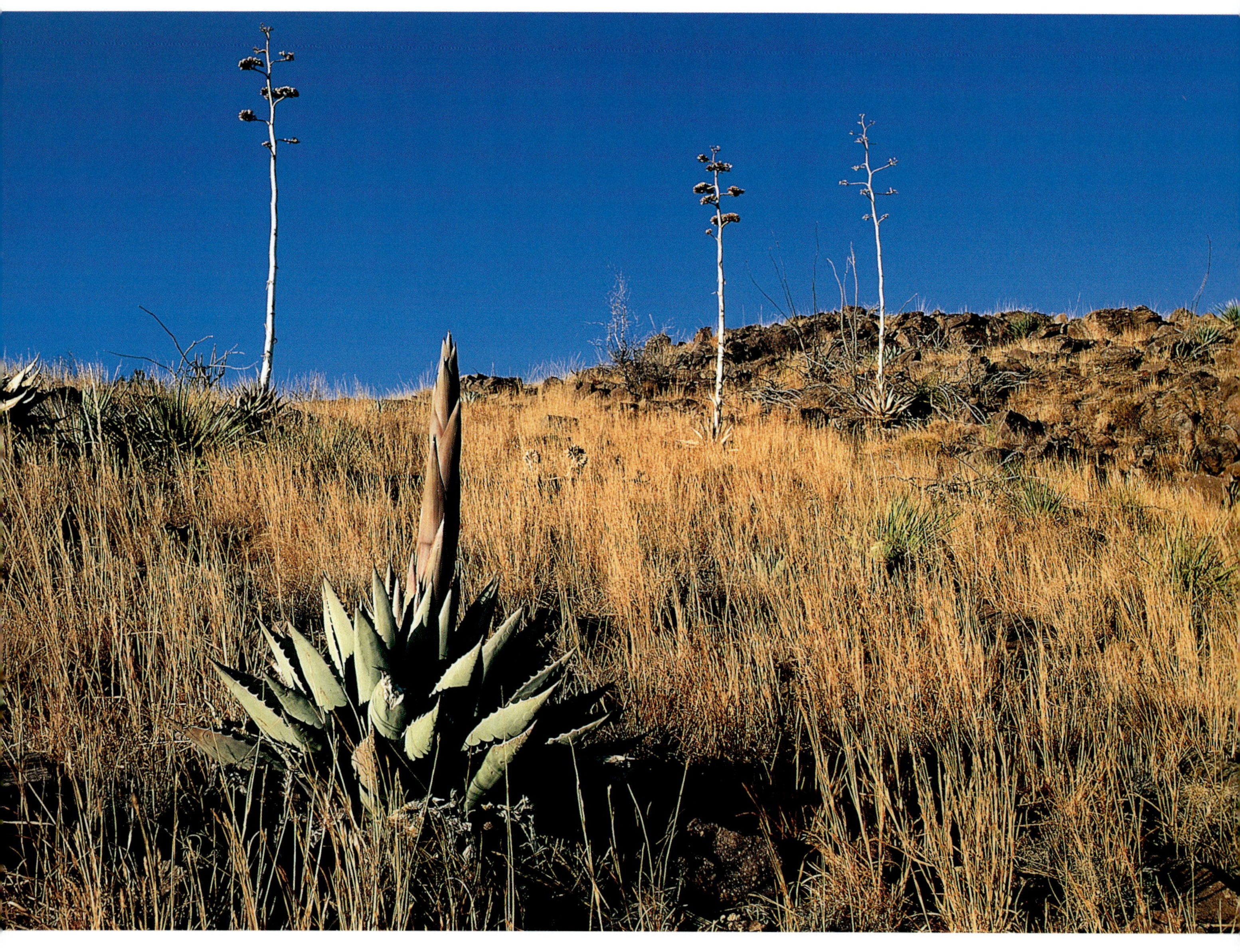

DESERT SANCTUARIES

2

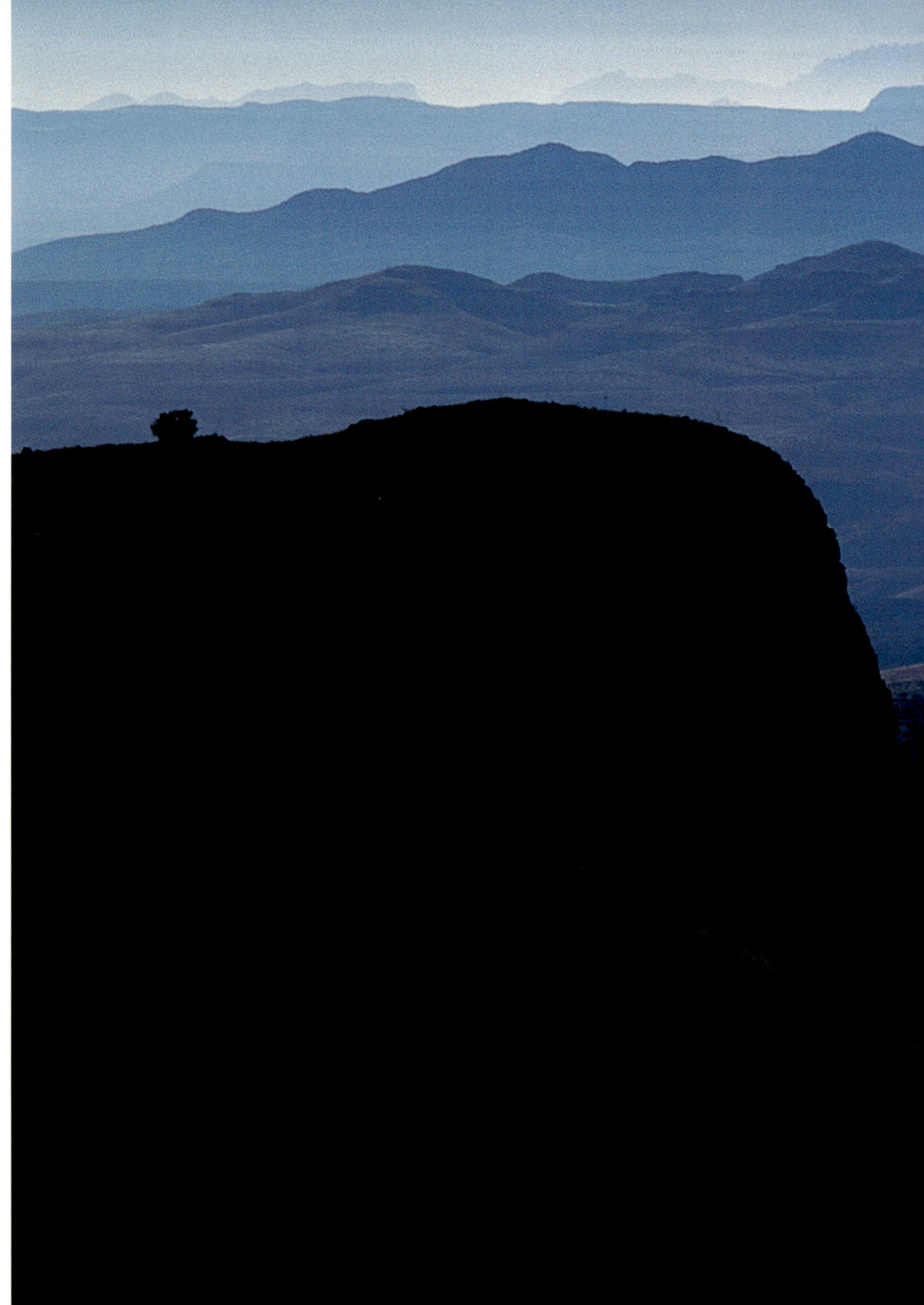

From Chinati Peak,
looking toward the Chisos
at sunrise

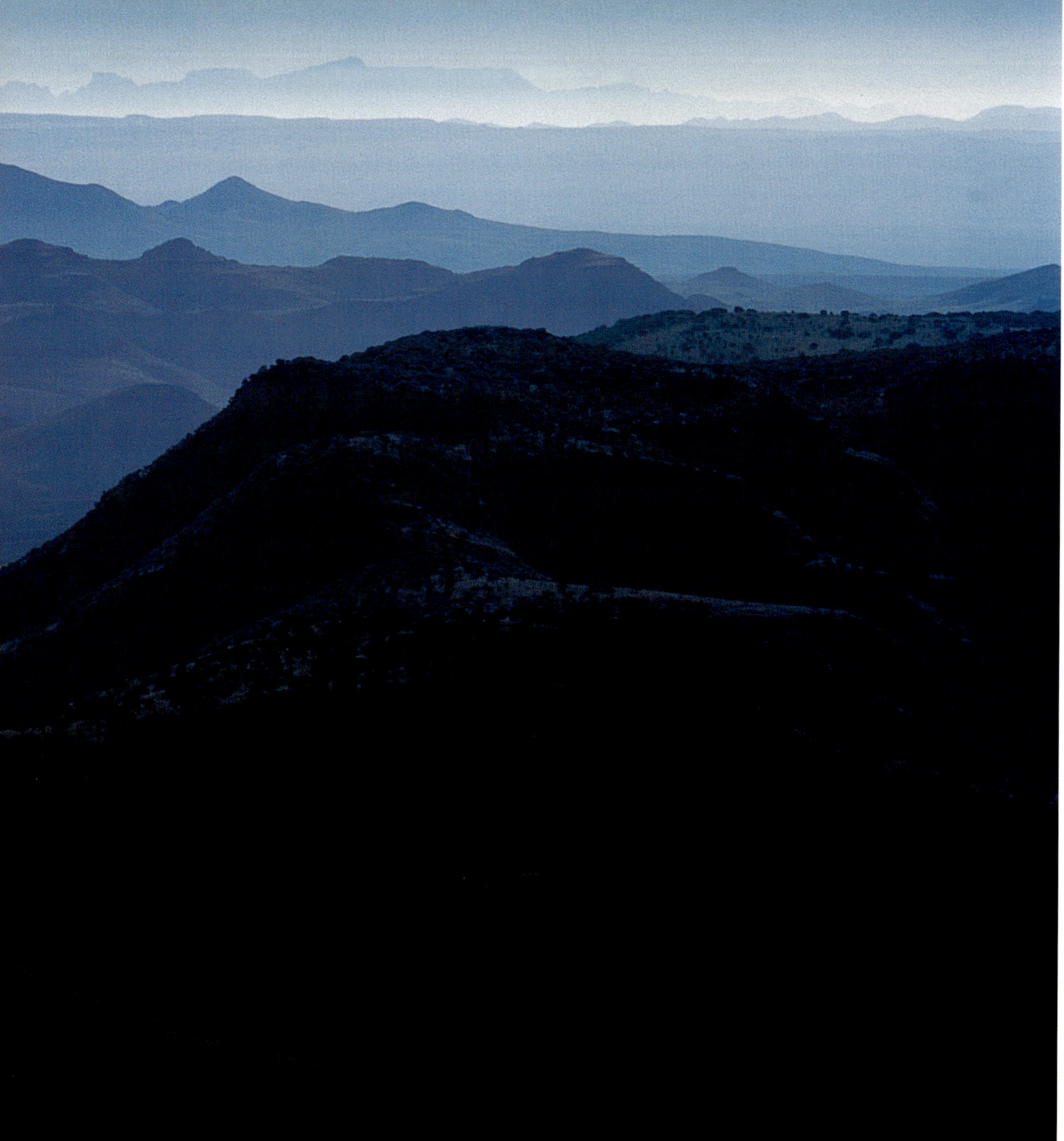

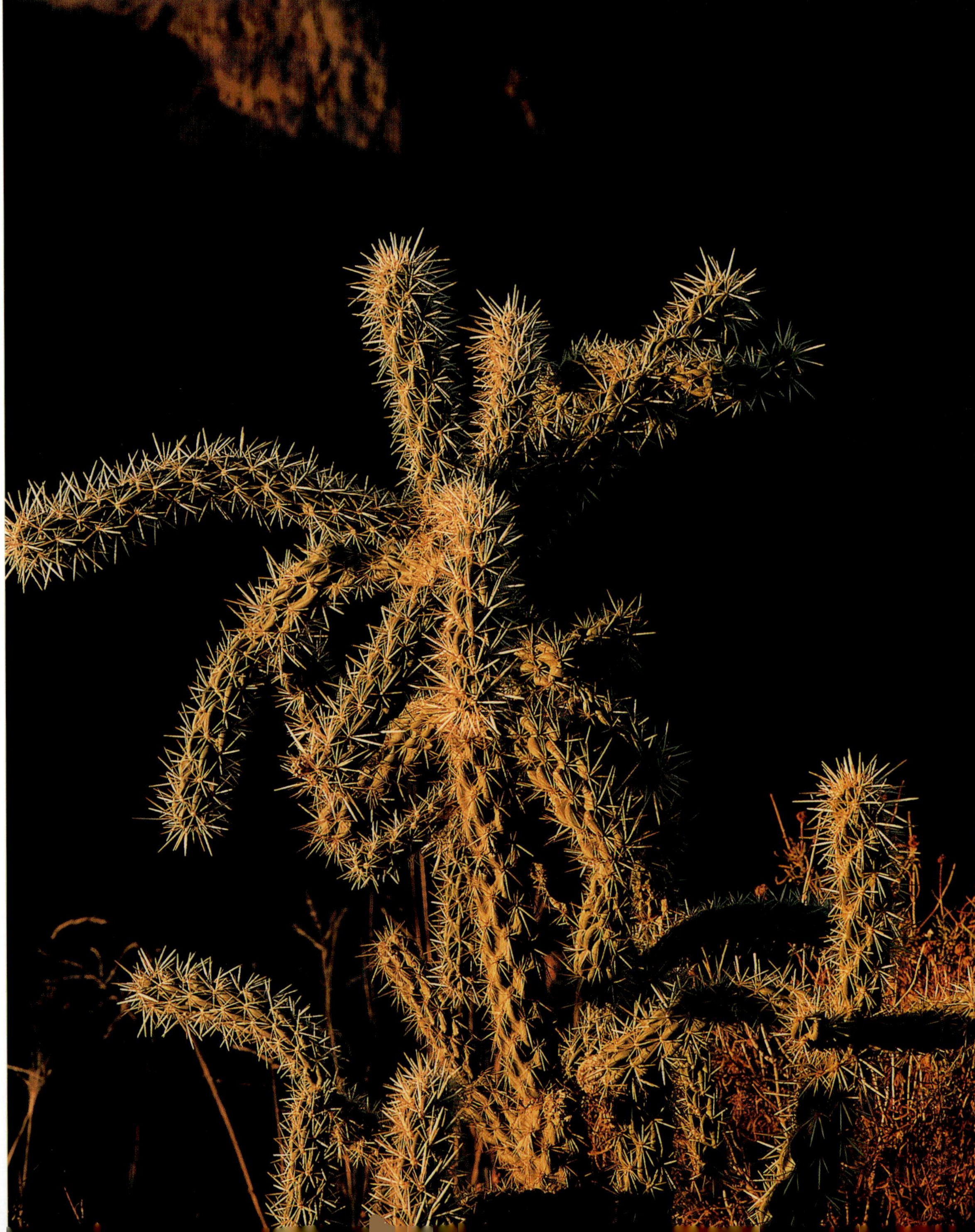

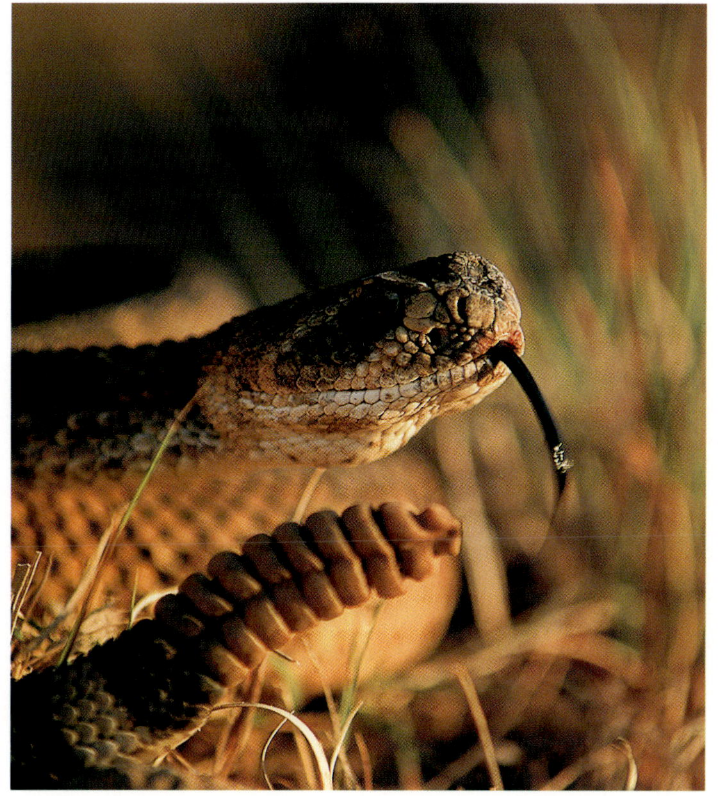

OPPOSITE: Cholla, eastern rim of Pelillos Canyon, late afternoon

ABOVE: Western diamondback

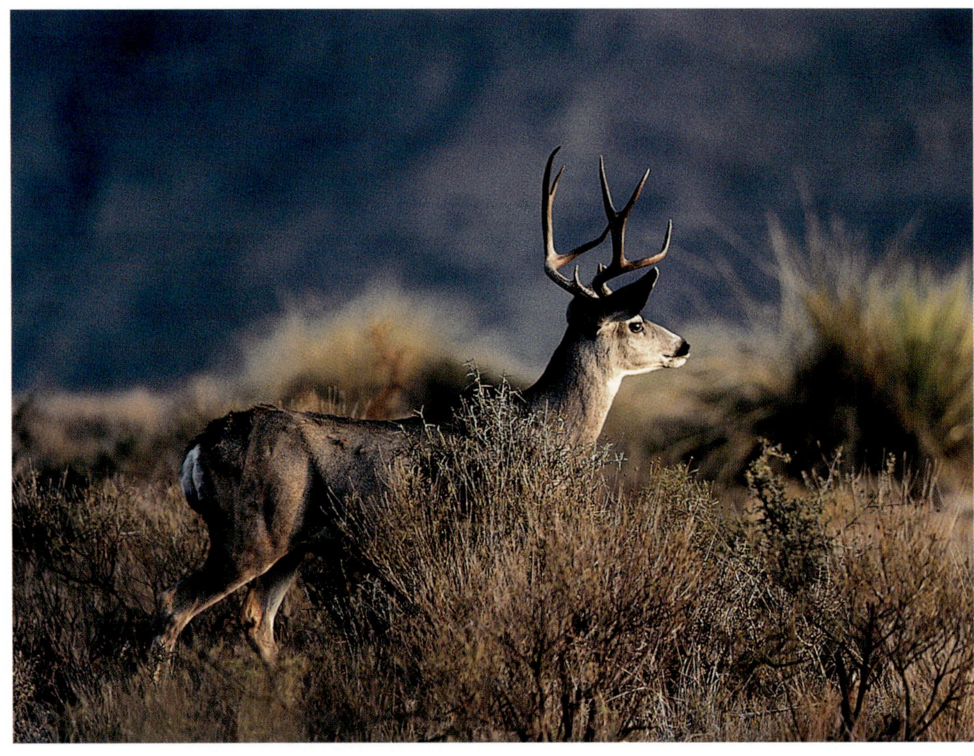

OPPOSITE: Southern view of western rim of San Antonio Canyon, looking into Mexico

ABOVE: Desert muledeer

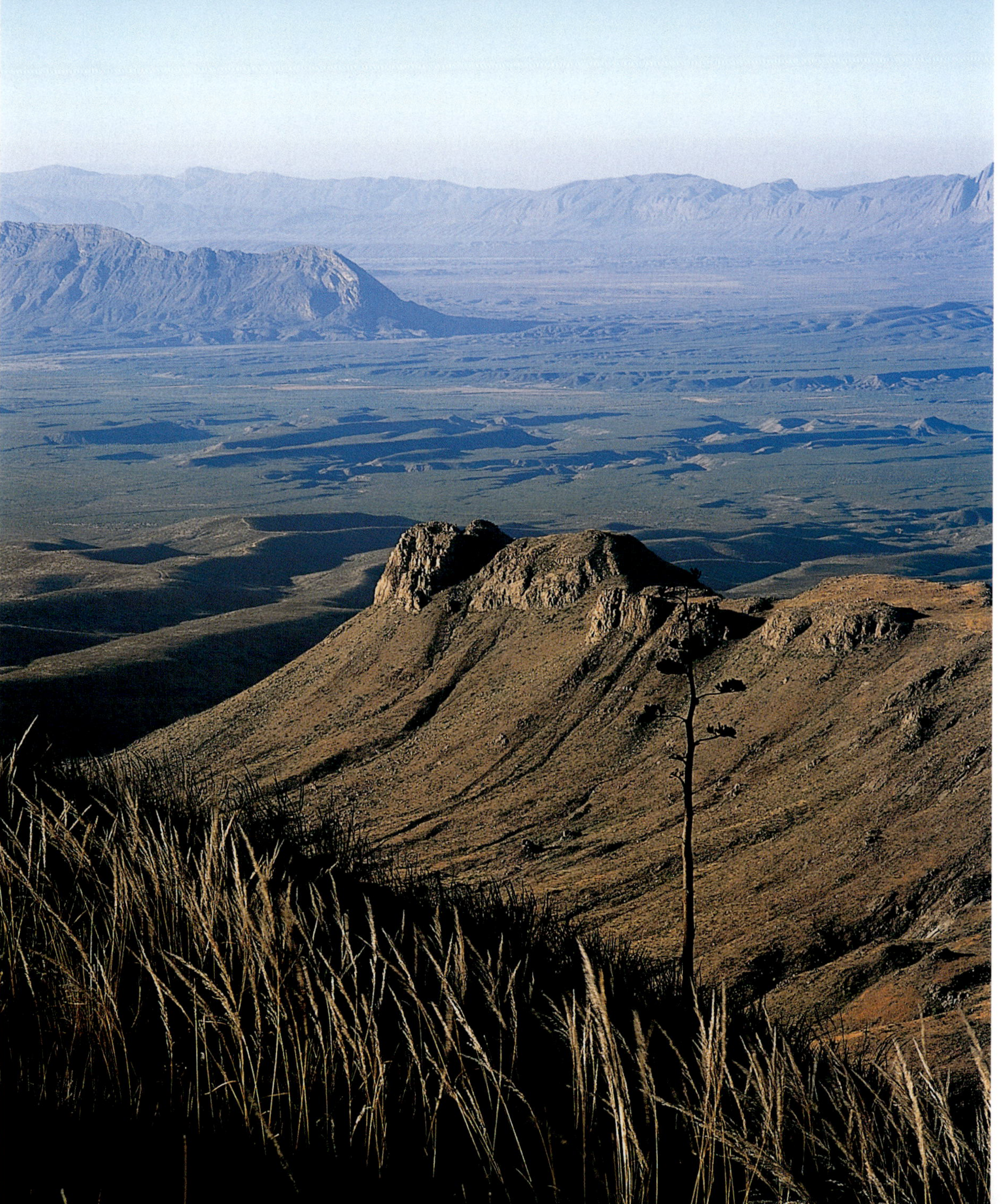

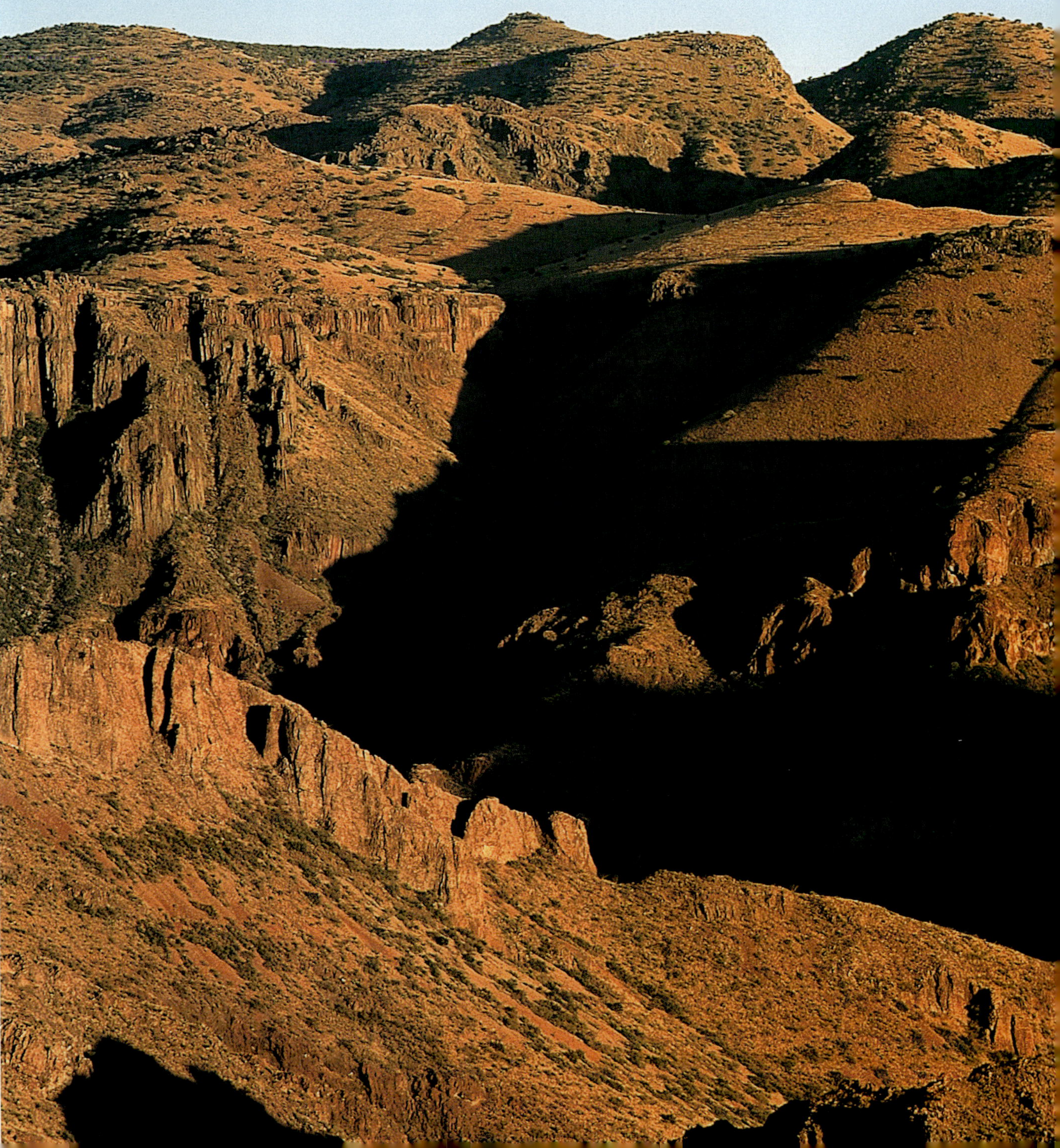

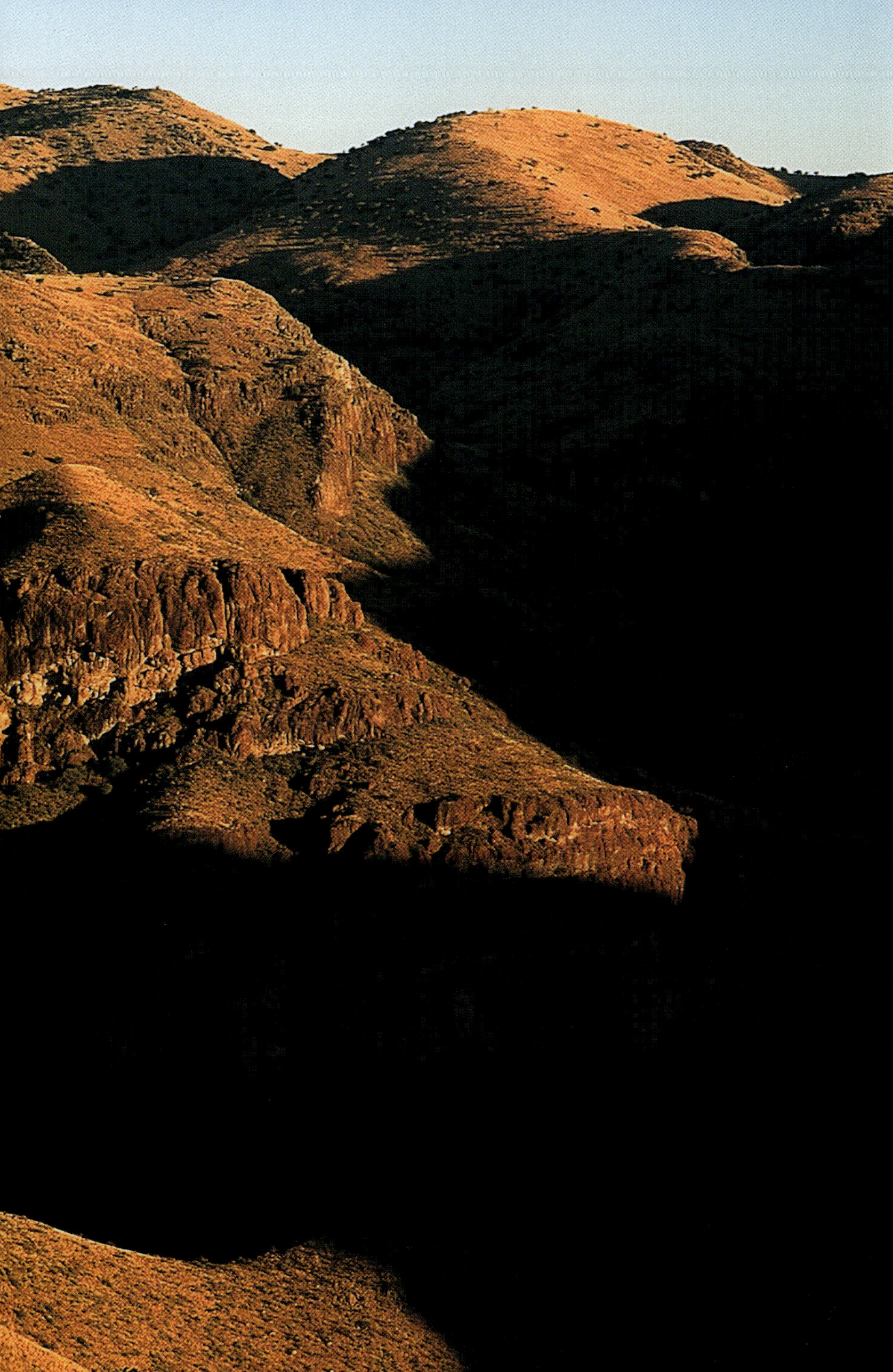

Pelillos Canyon, looking east

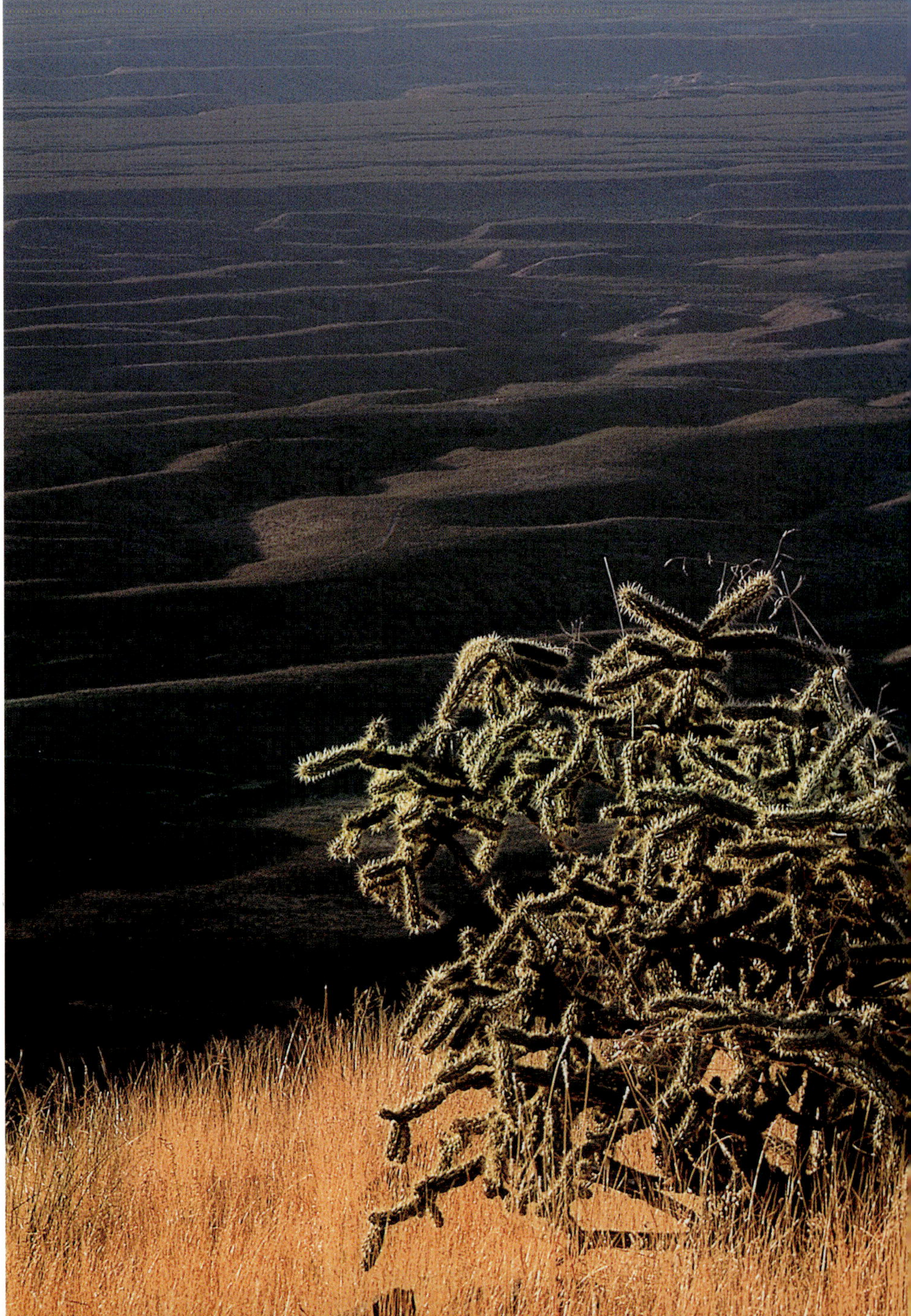

Cholla at sunrise, eastern rim of San Antonio Canyon, looking south

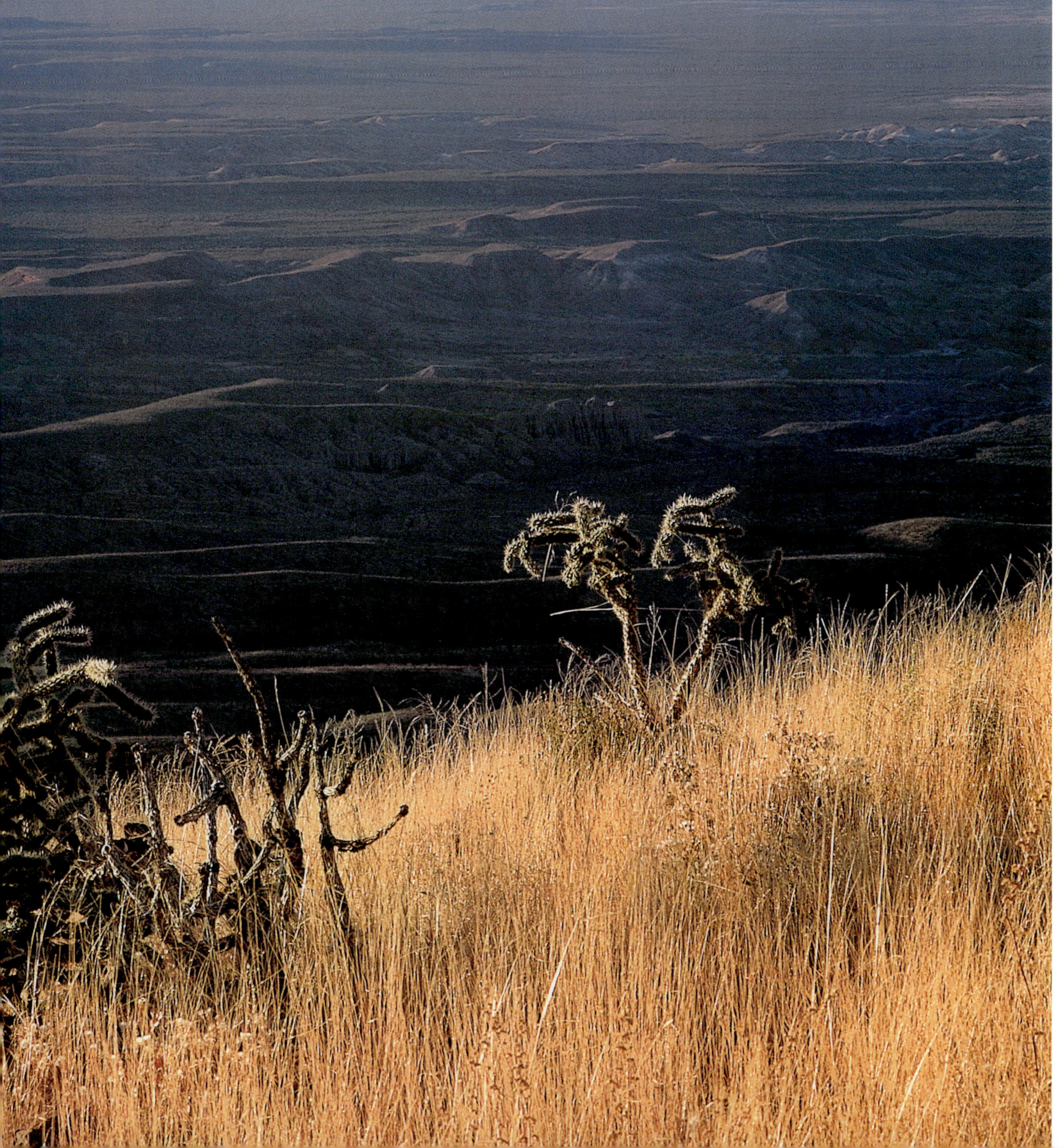

Benches below Chinati Peak
at sunrise

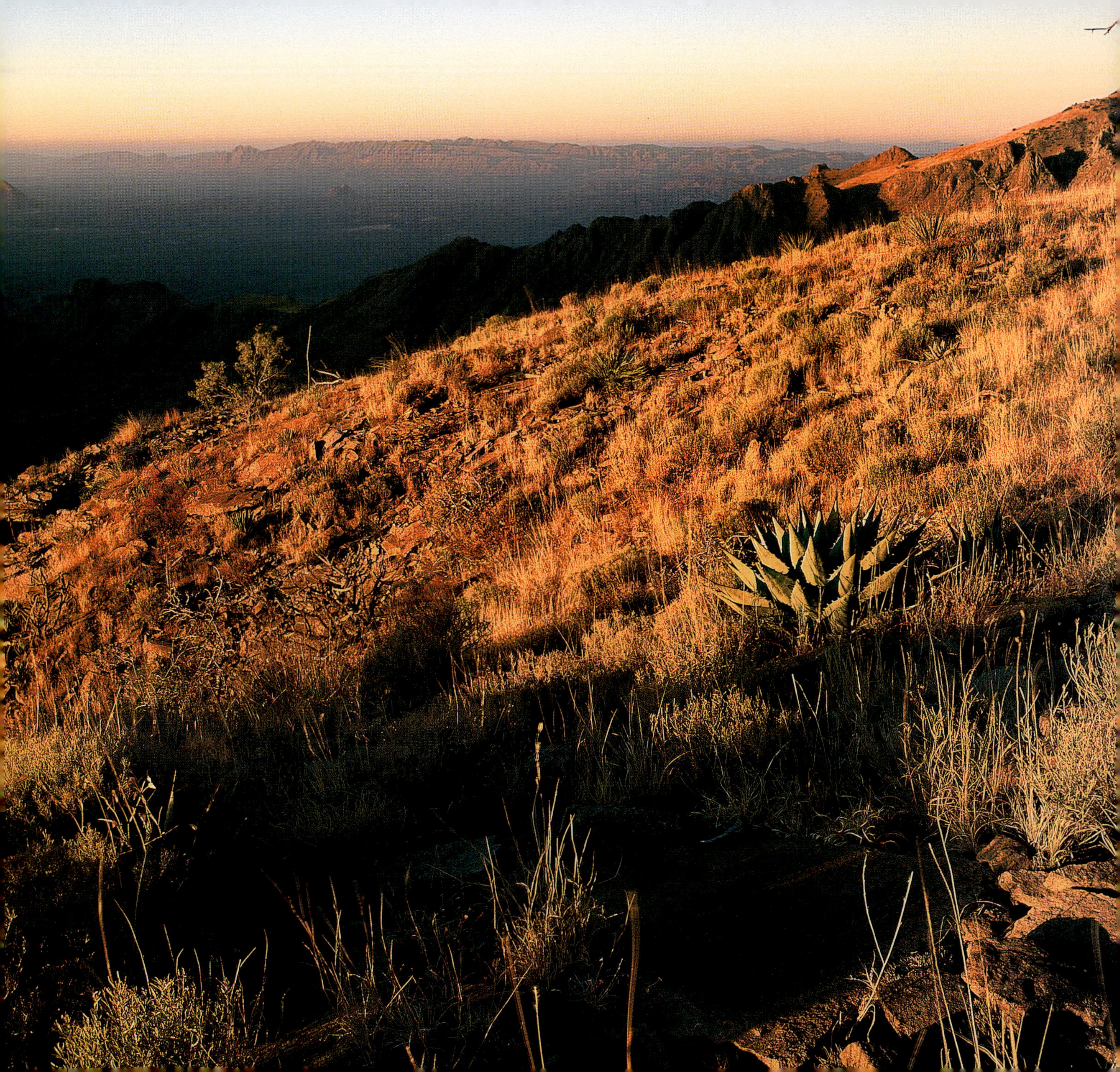

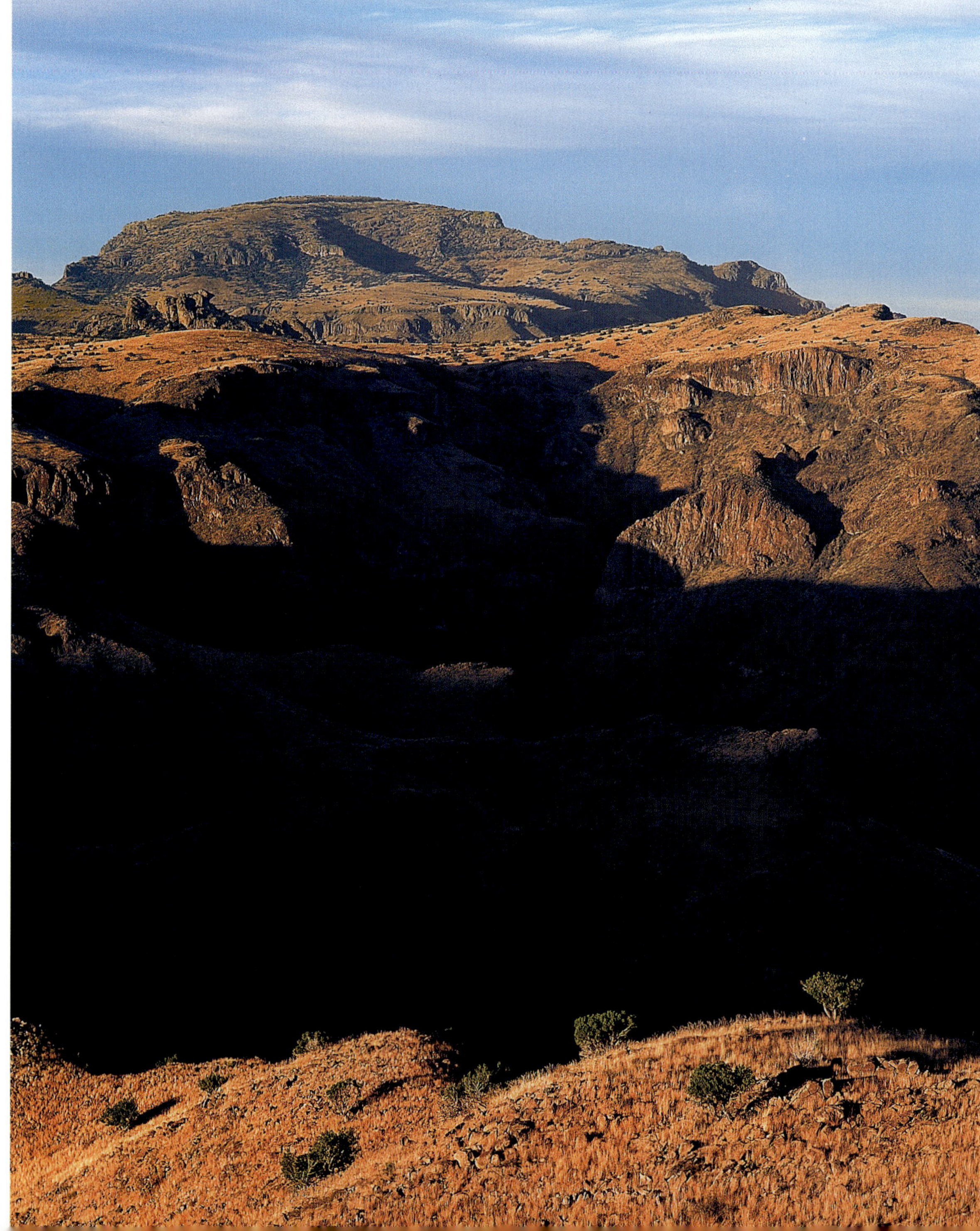

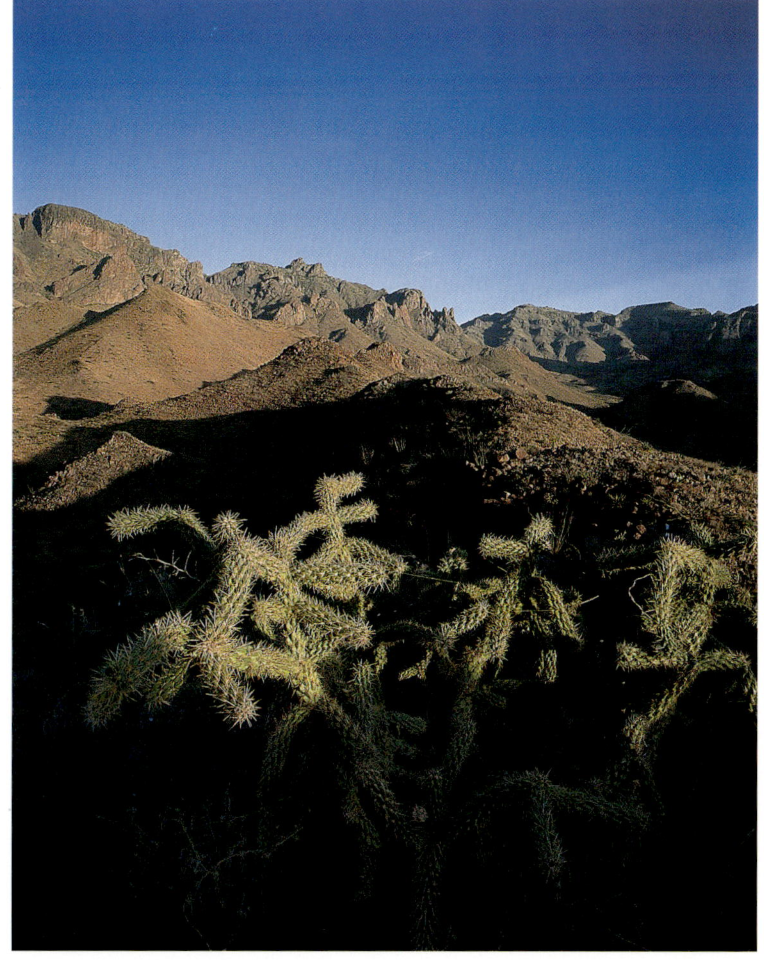

OPPOSITE: Eastern rim of Pelillos Canyon at sunrise, looking north

ABOVE: The mouth of San Antonio Canyon, late afternoon

Tinajas in Pelillos Canyon,
looking northwest,
before sunset

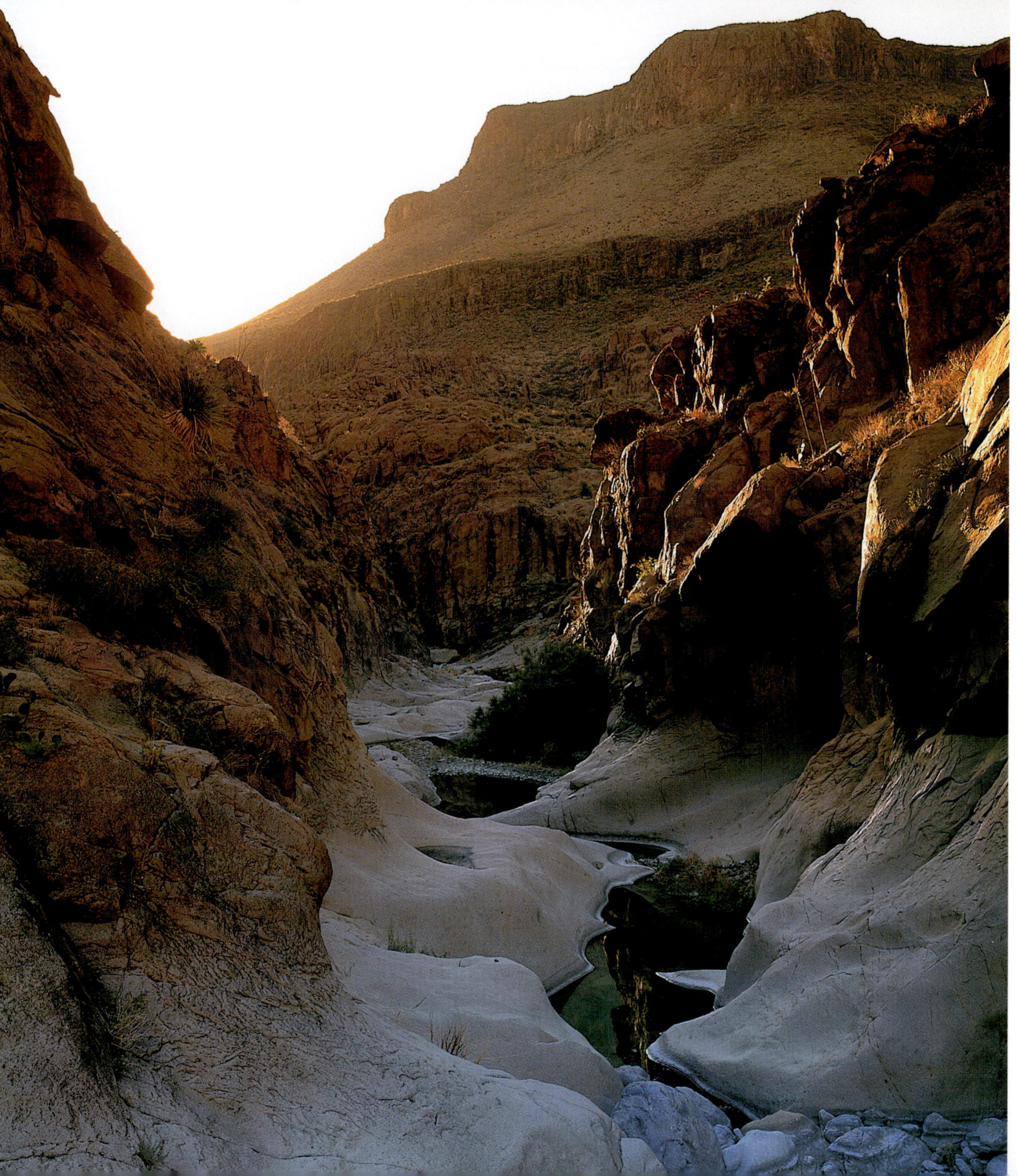

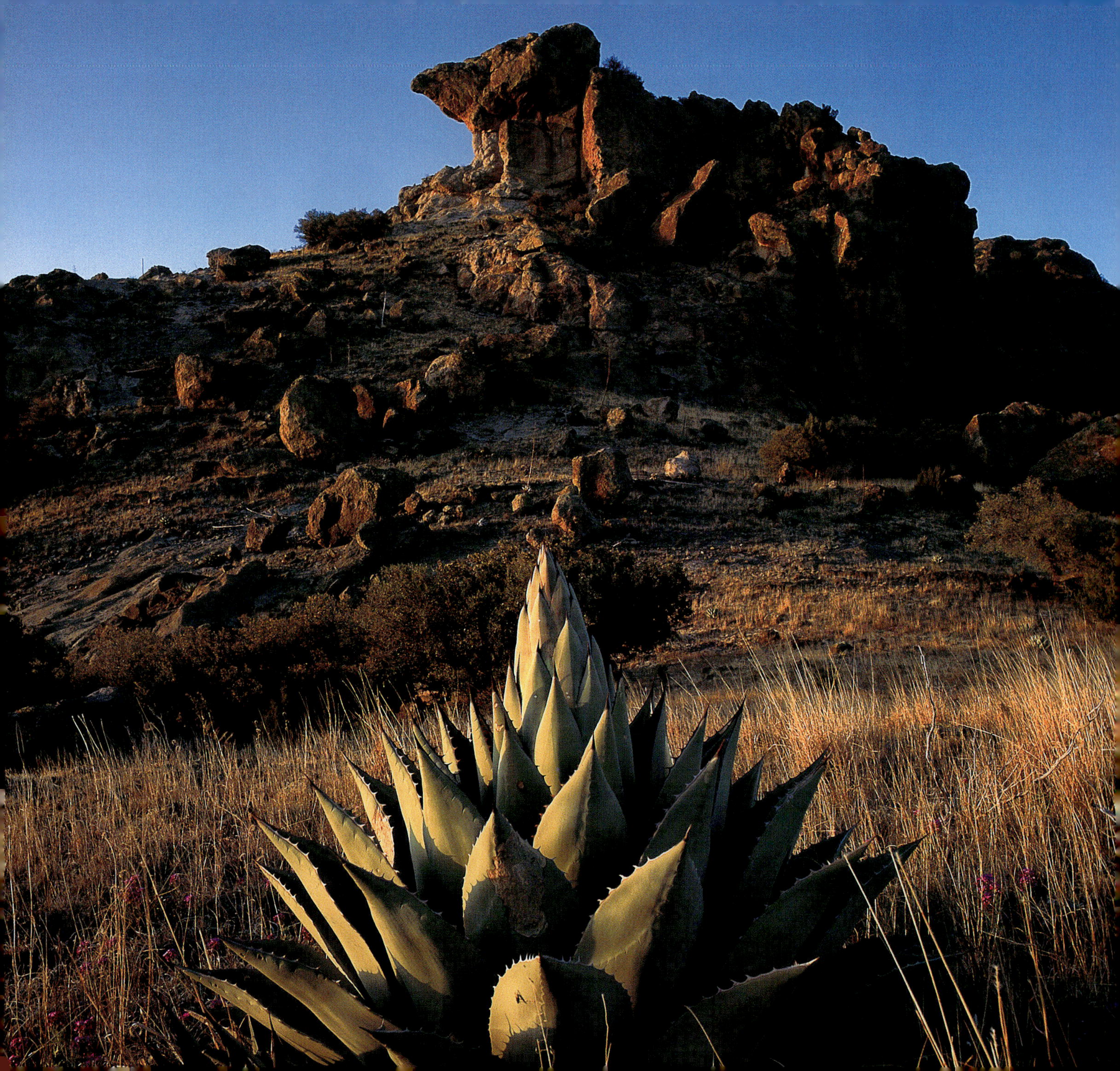

Eastern rim of San Antonio Canyon, late evening, looking north

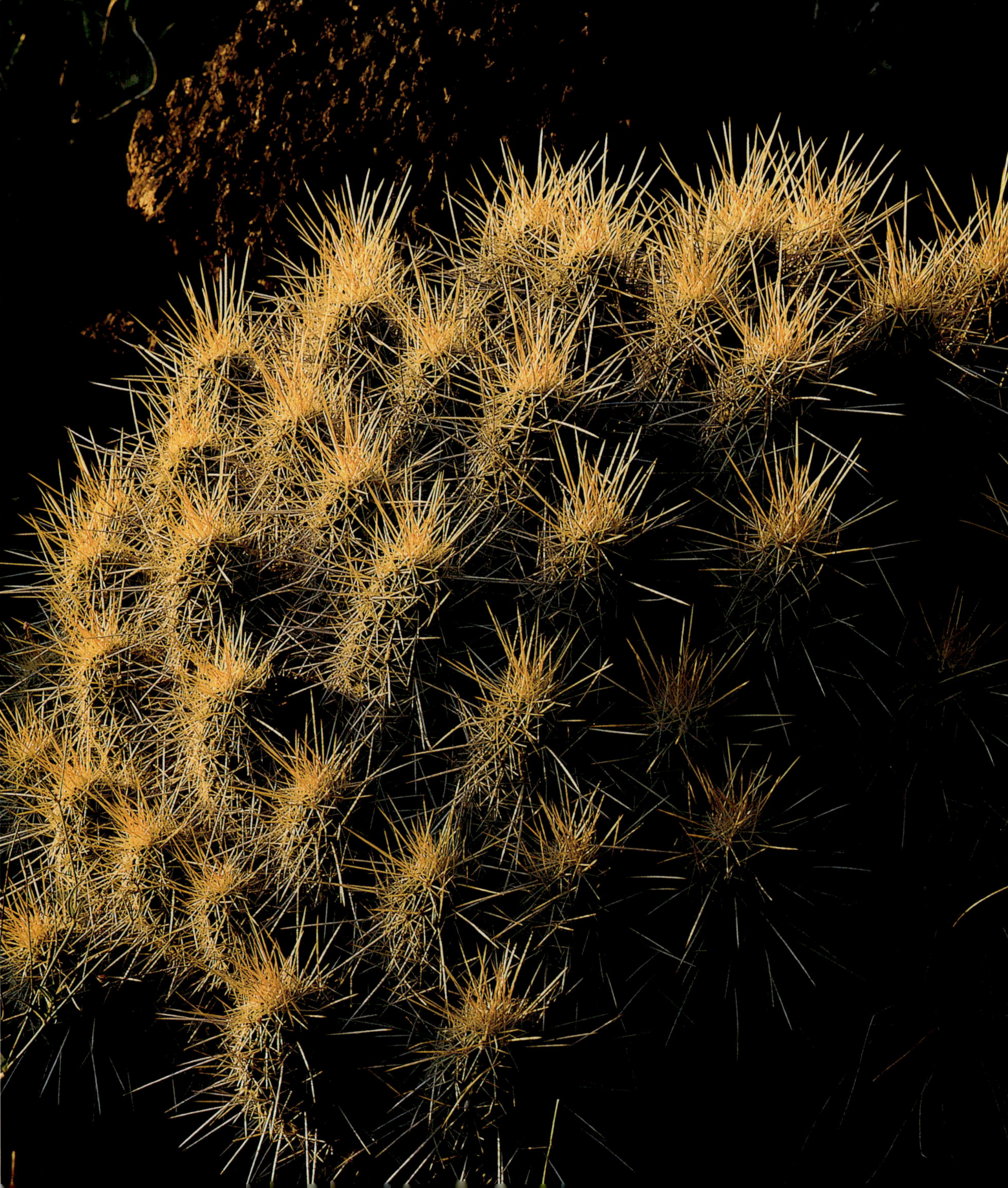

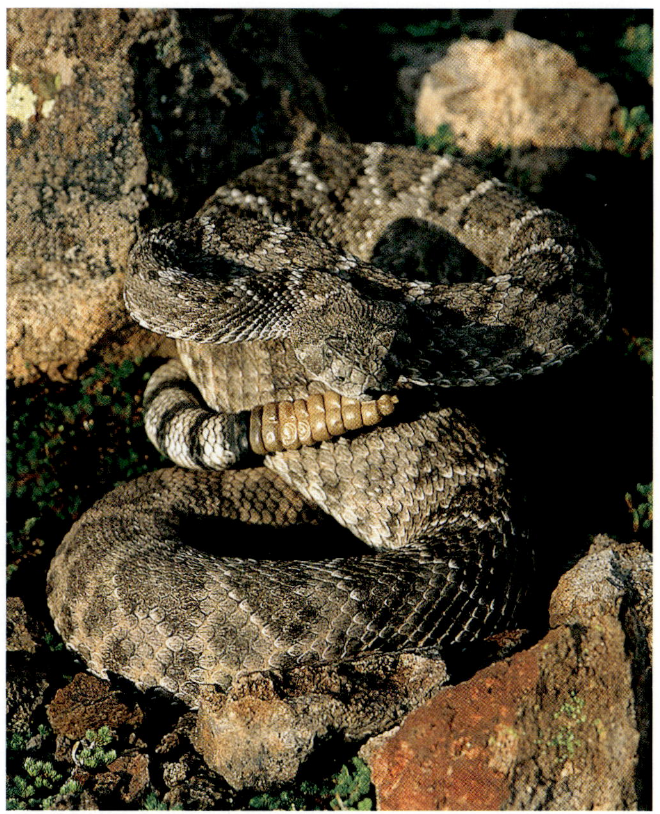

OPPOSITE: Strawberry cactus, eastern rim of San Antonio Canyon, late afternoon

ABOVE: Mojave rattlesnake

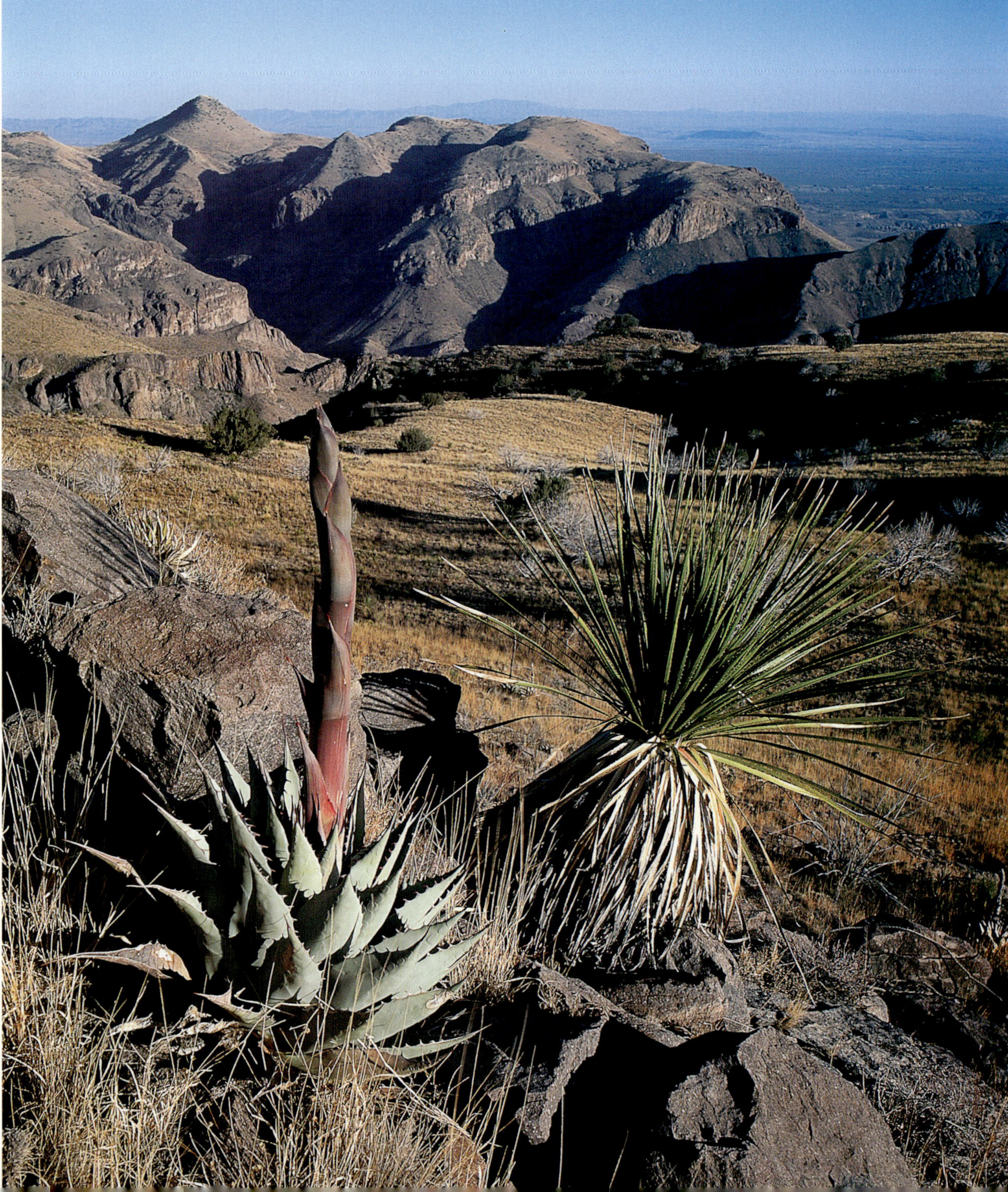

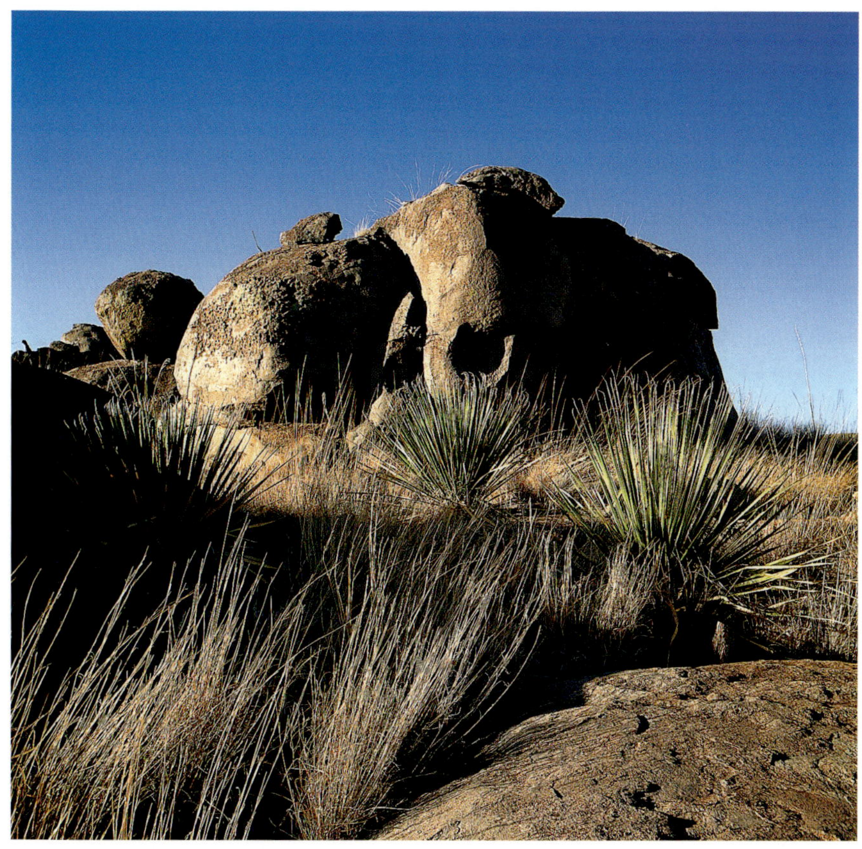

OPPOSITE: Southeastern edge of San Antonio Canyon, near mouth, looking southeast

ABOVE: Boulders, eastern rim of Pelillos Canyon, morning

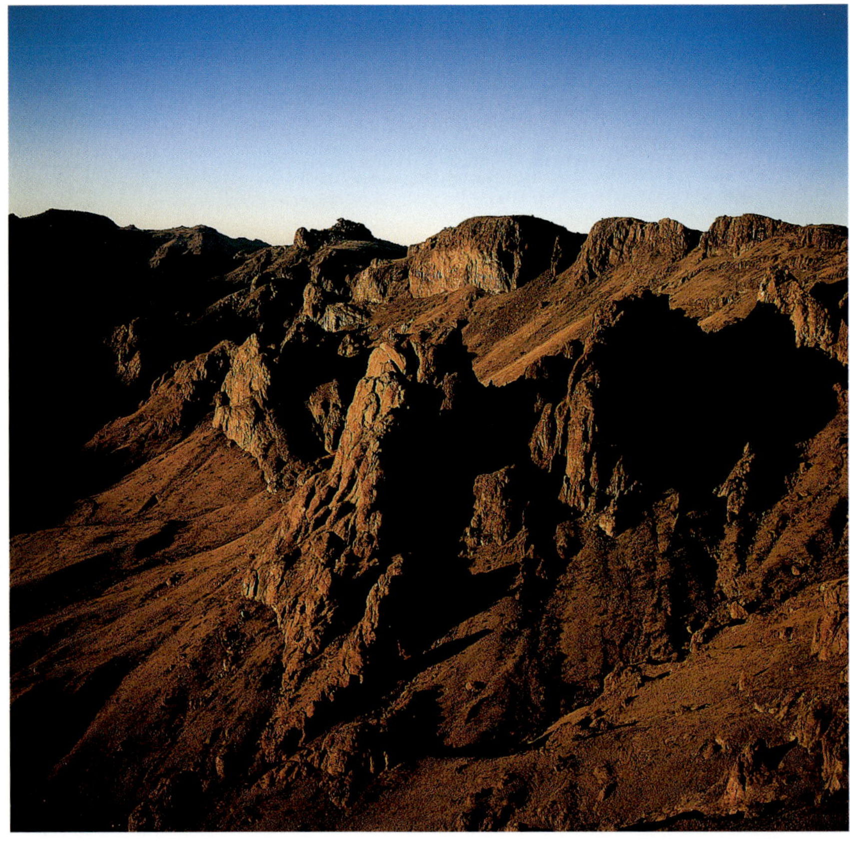

OPPOSITE: Southern edge of Chinatis escarpment, aerial view, looking north

ABOVE: Eastern slopes of San Antonio Canyon, looking north up San Antonio Canyon, late afternoon

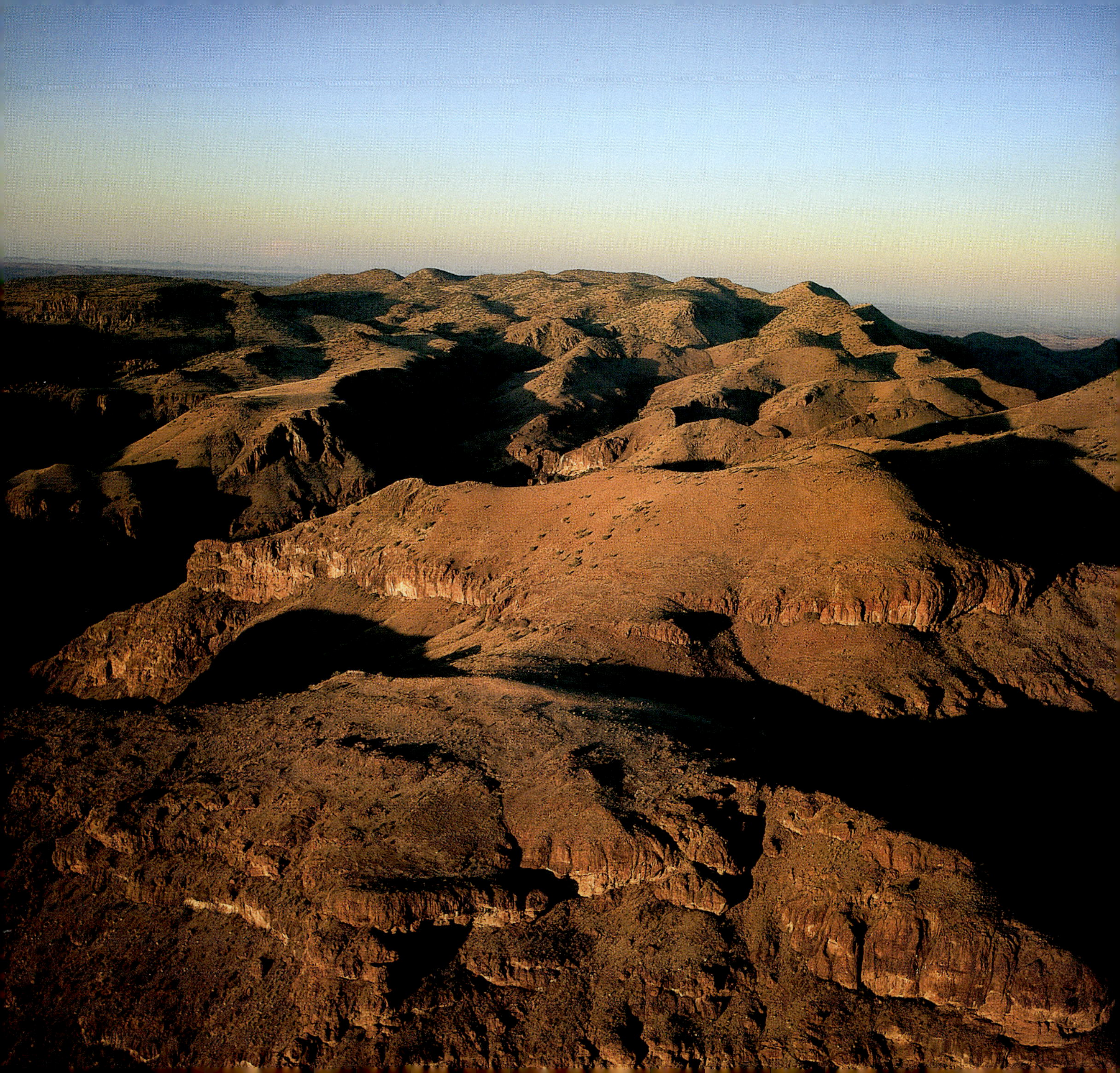

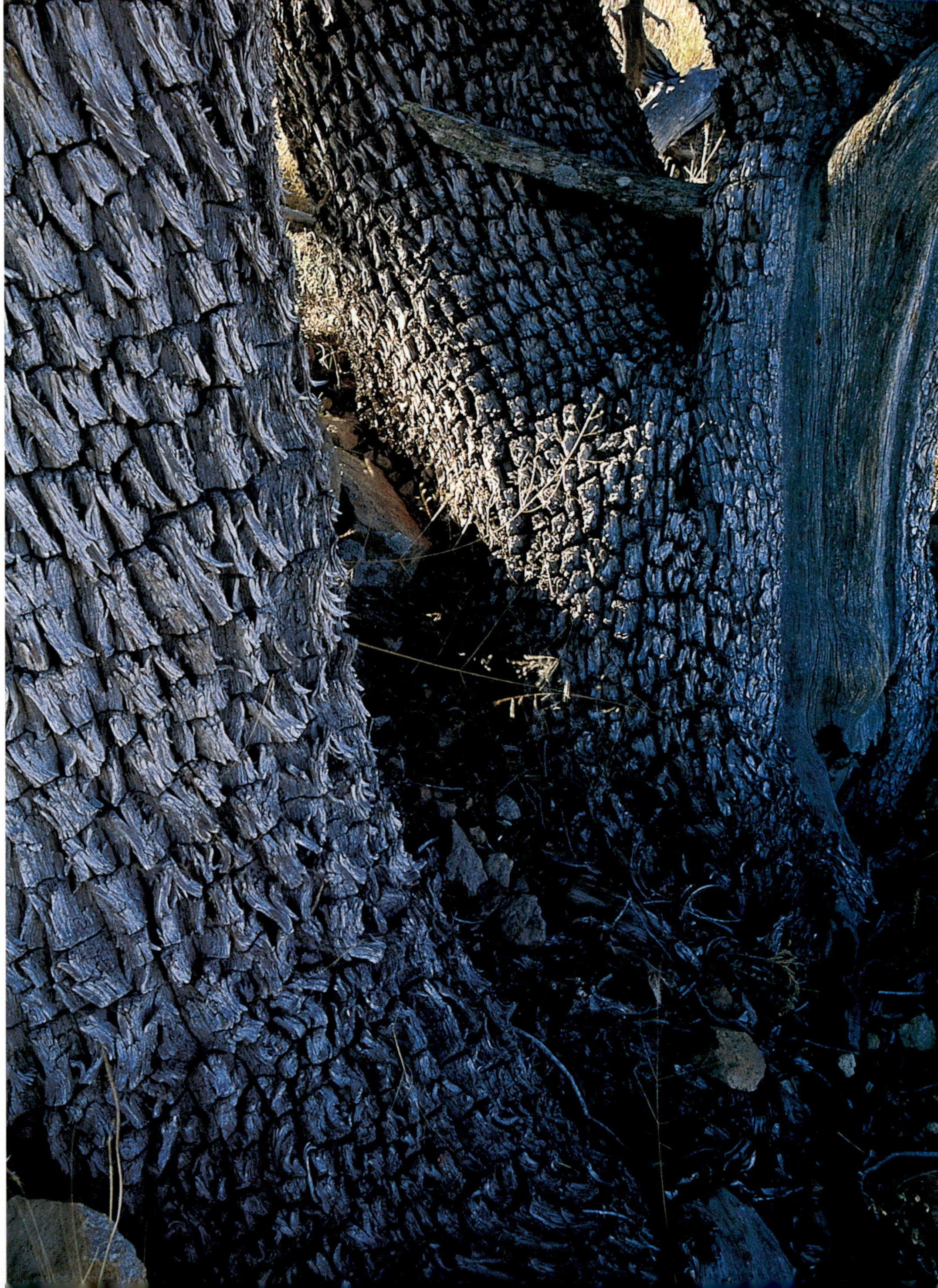

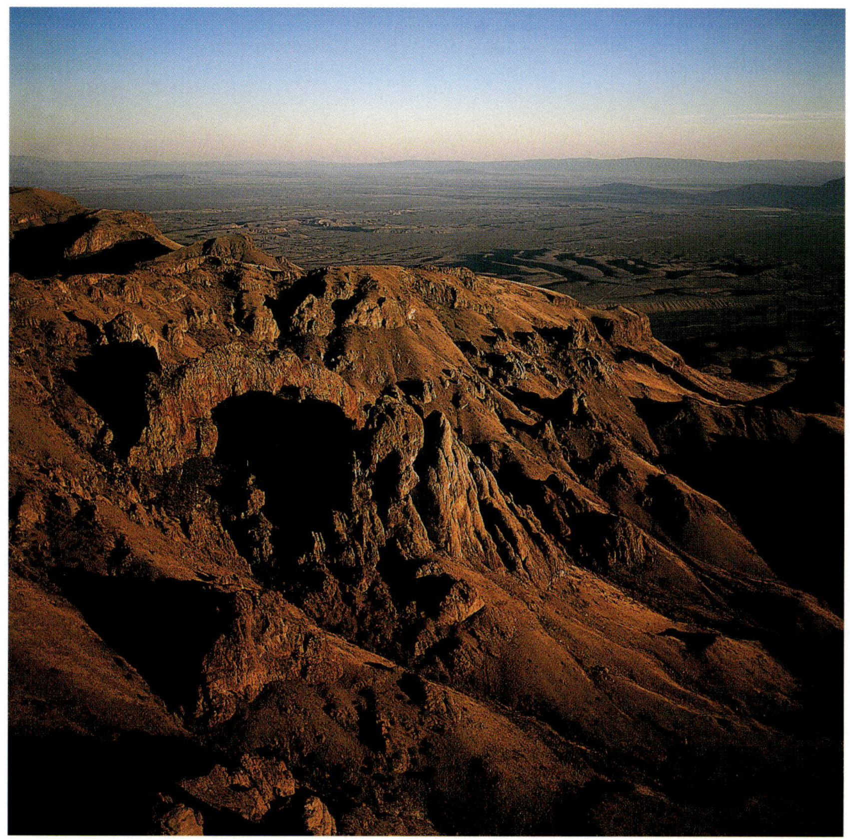

OPPOSITE: Trunks of alligator juniper near summit of Chinati Peak, early morning

ABOVE: Eastern slopes, mouth of San Antonio Canyon, looking southeast, aerial shot

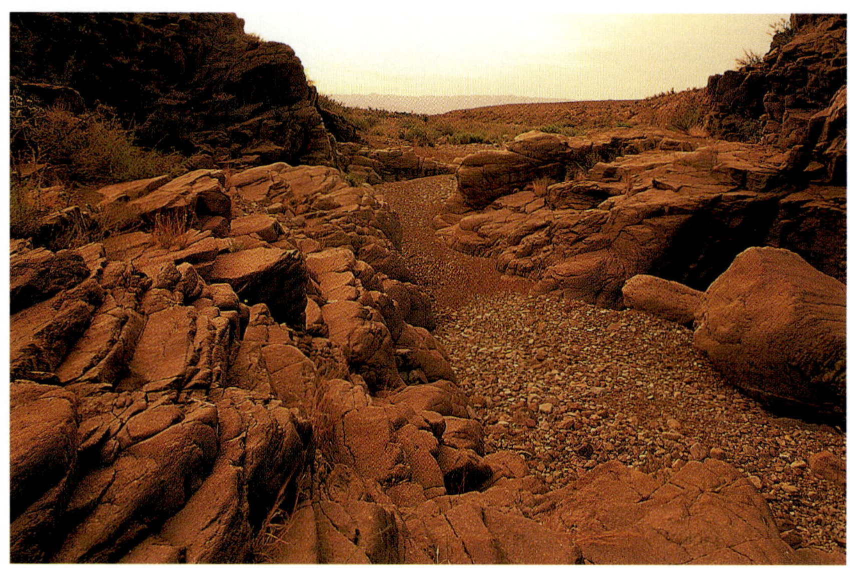

OPPOSITE: Eastern slopes of Chinati Mountains, from Shafter, sunrise

ABOVE: Mouth of Pelillos Canyon, sunset

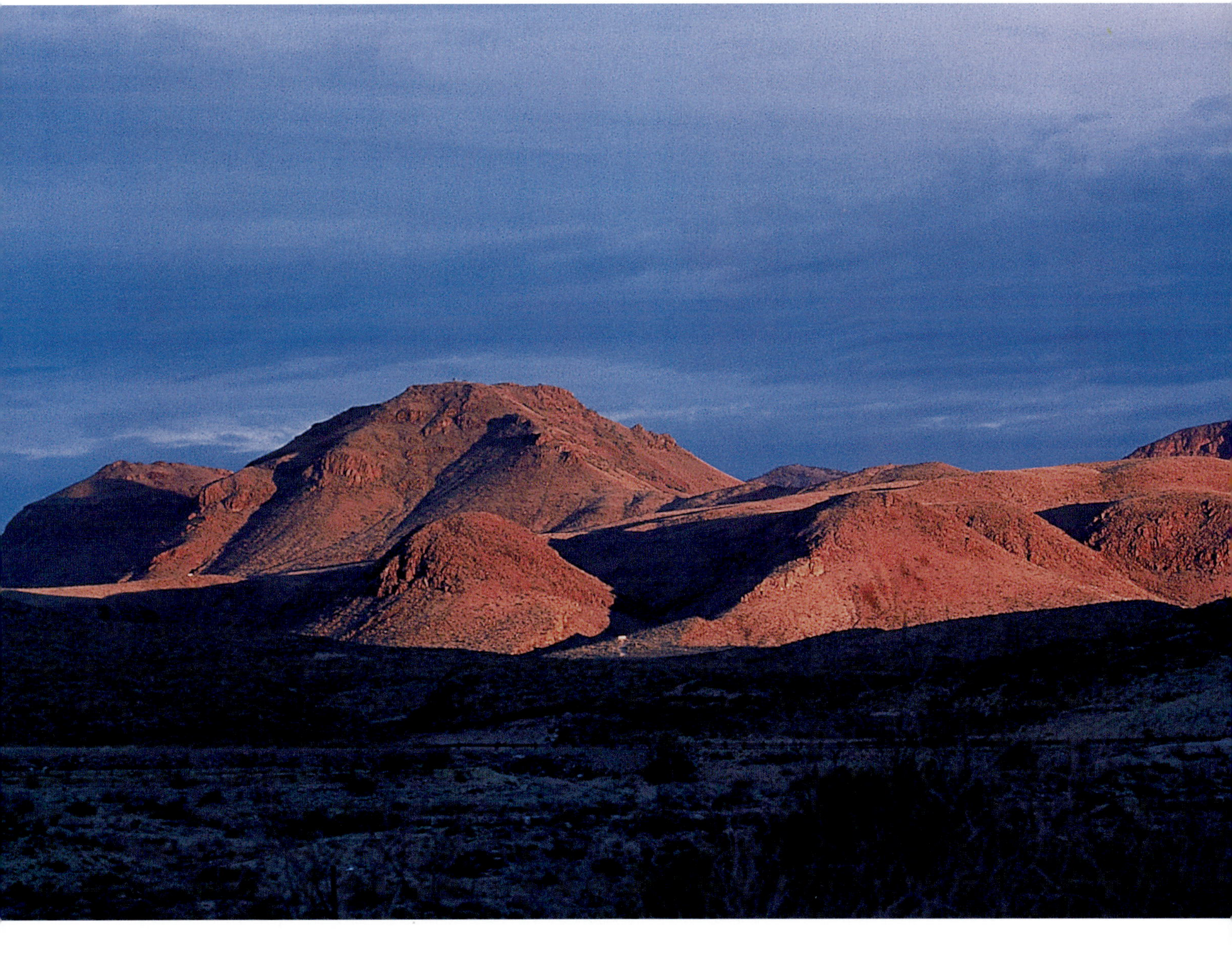

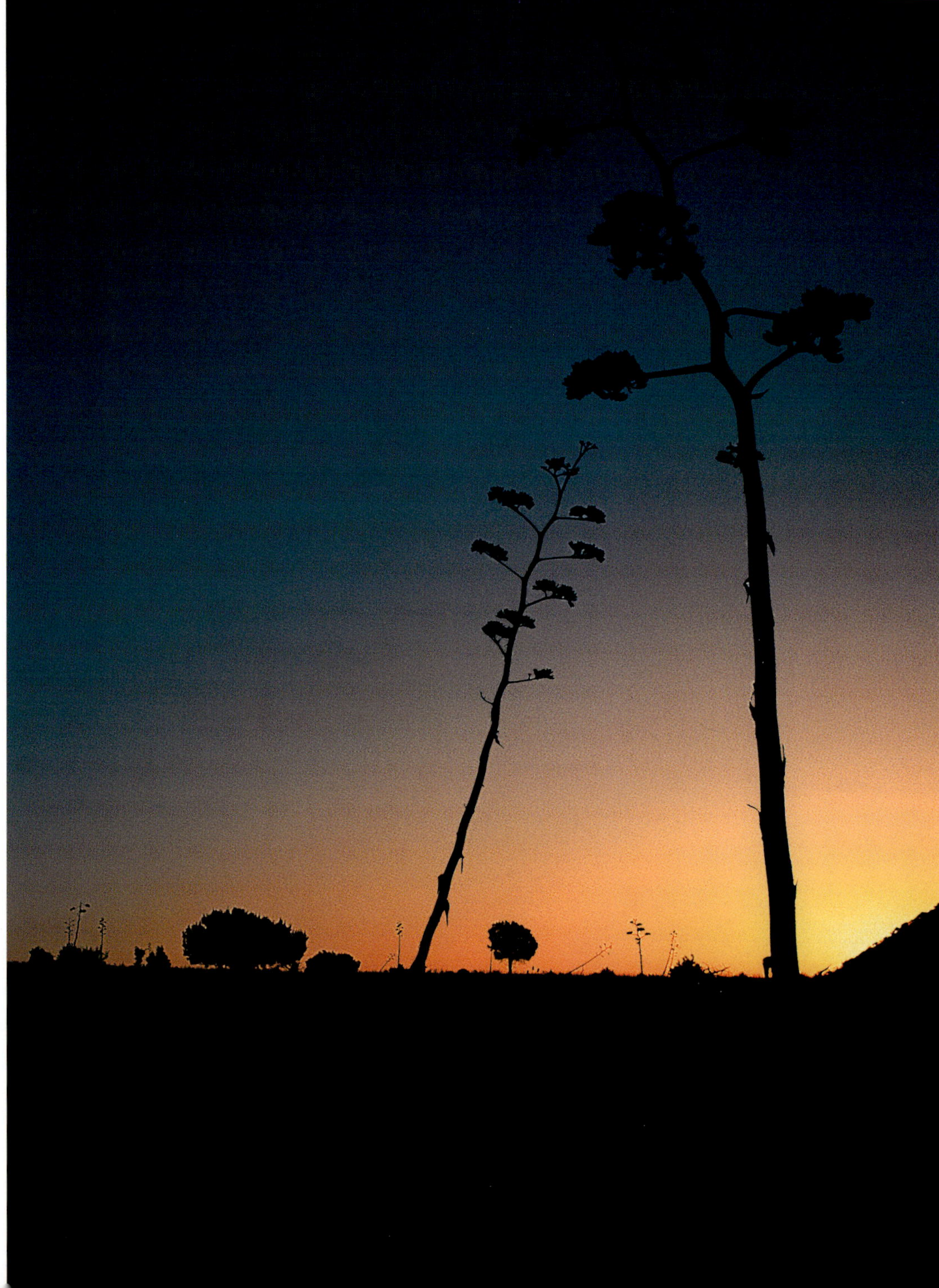

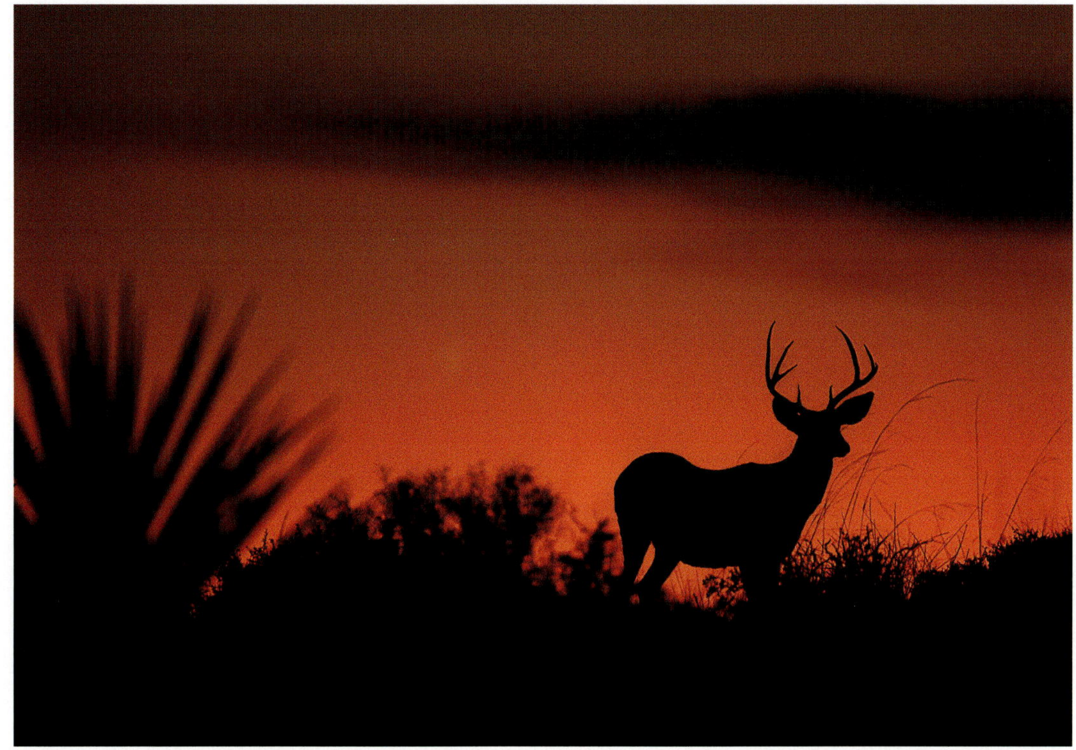

OPPOSITE: Agave flats, cresting eastern rim of San Antonio Canyon, looking east, morning

ABOVE: Desert muledeer

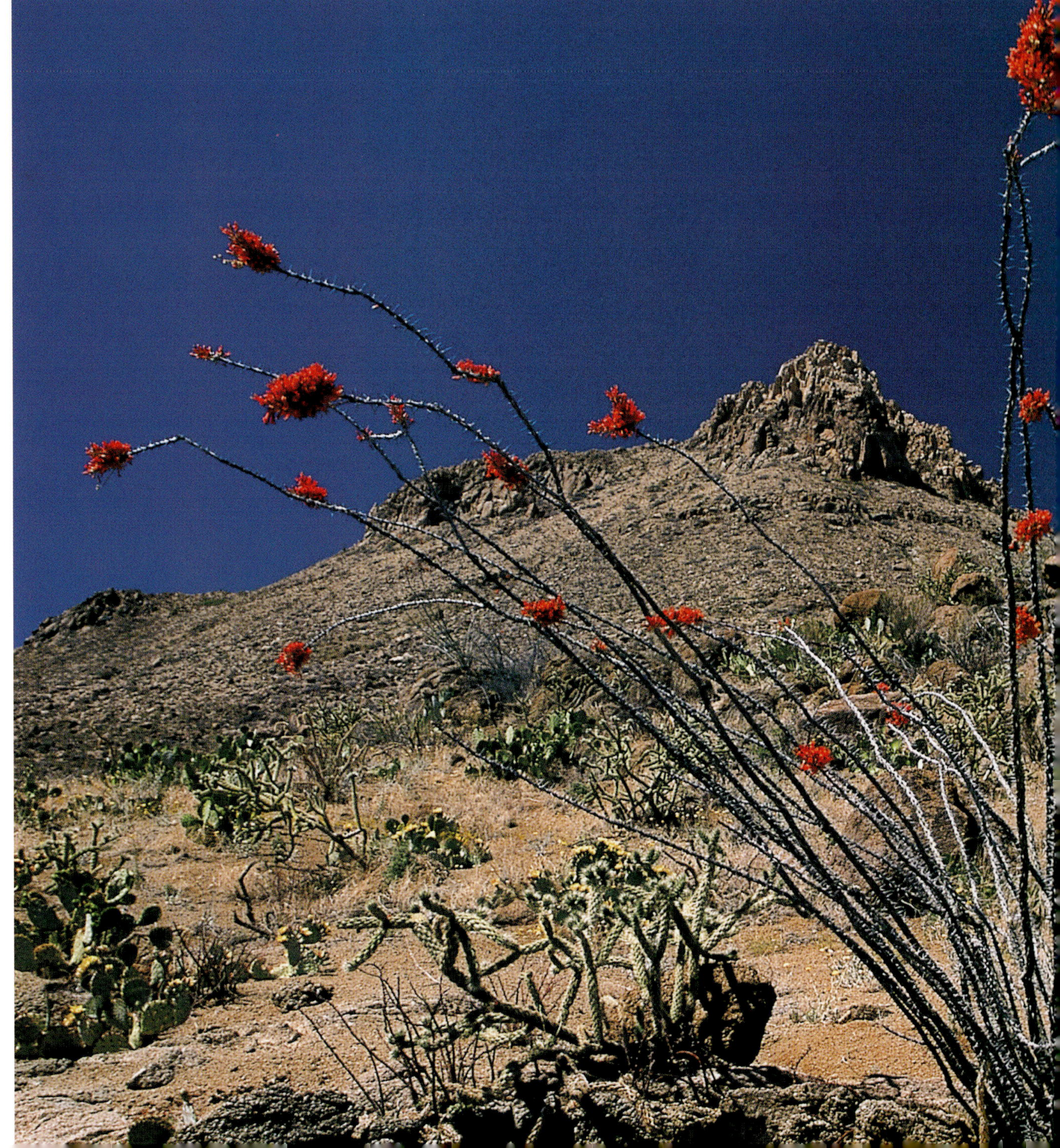

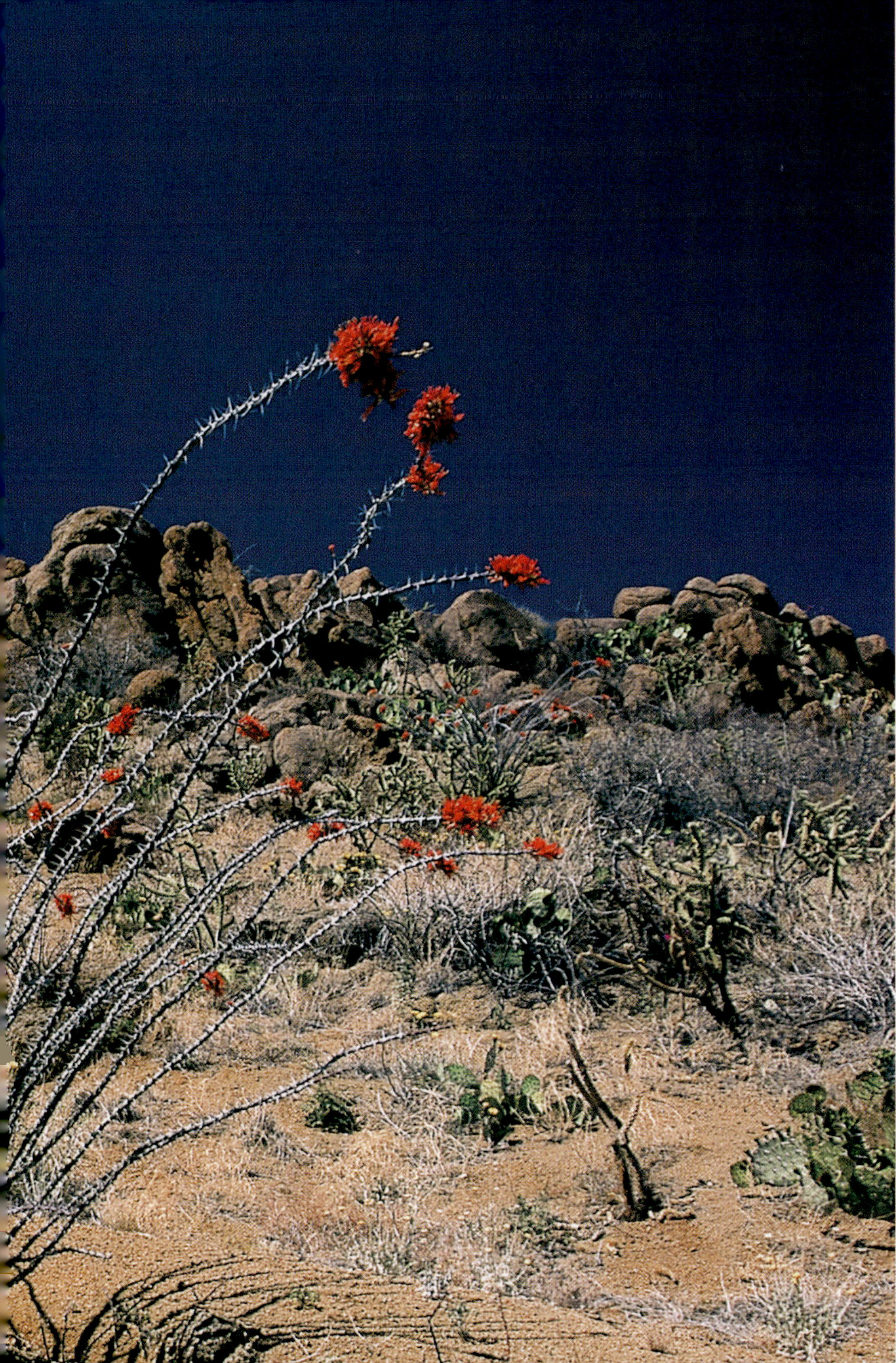

Blooming ocotillo, mouth of San Antonio Canyon, morning

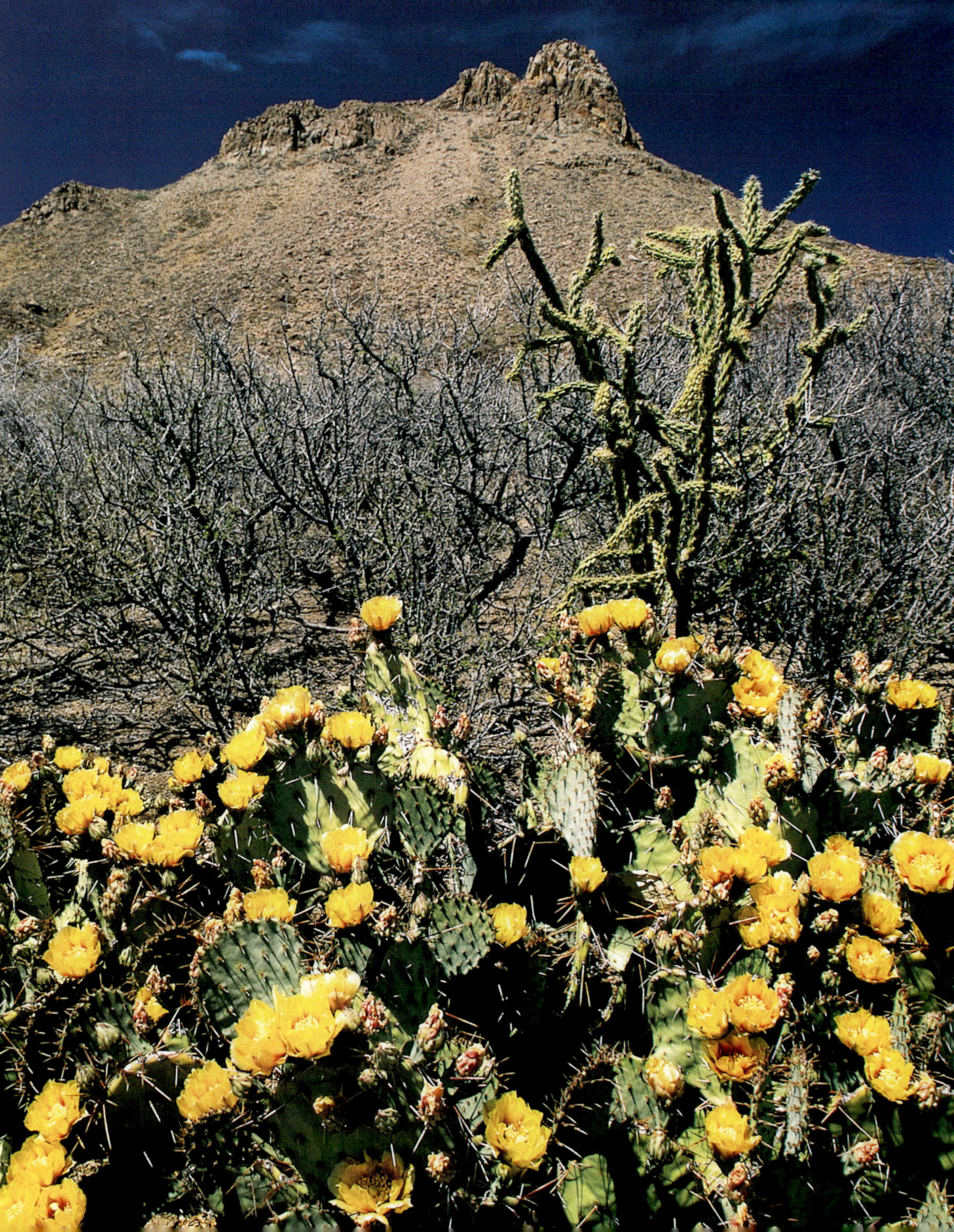

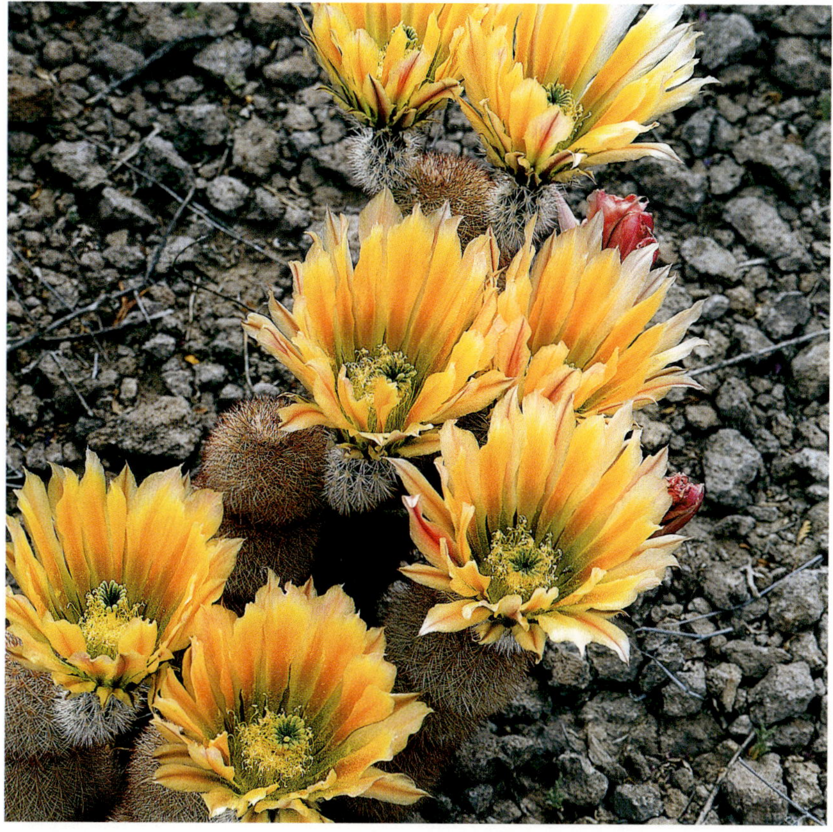

OPPOSITE: Prickly pear blossoms, San Antonio Canyon, morning

ABOVE: Rainbow cactus flowers near Cinco Tinajas, midday

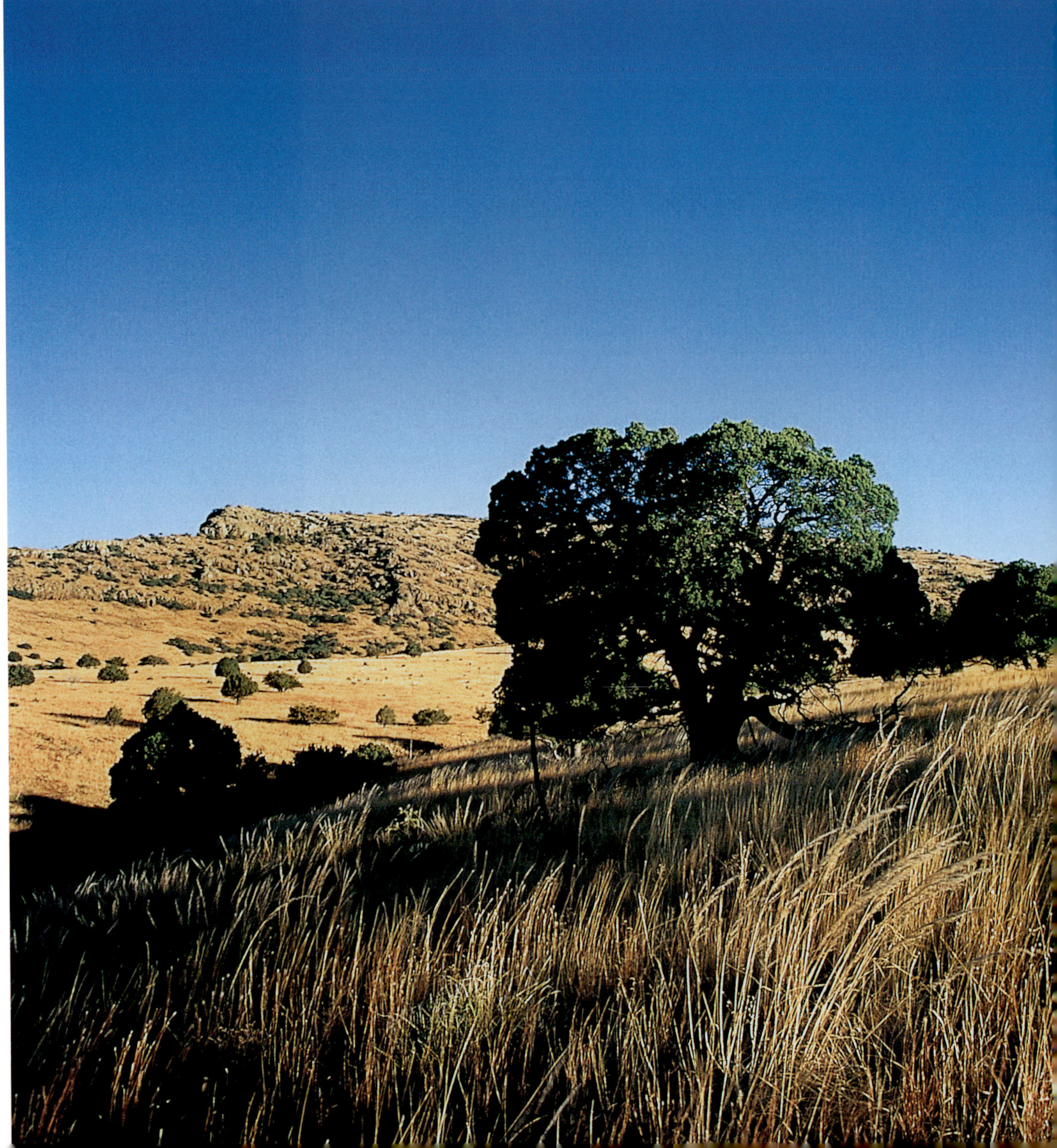

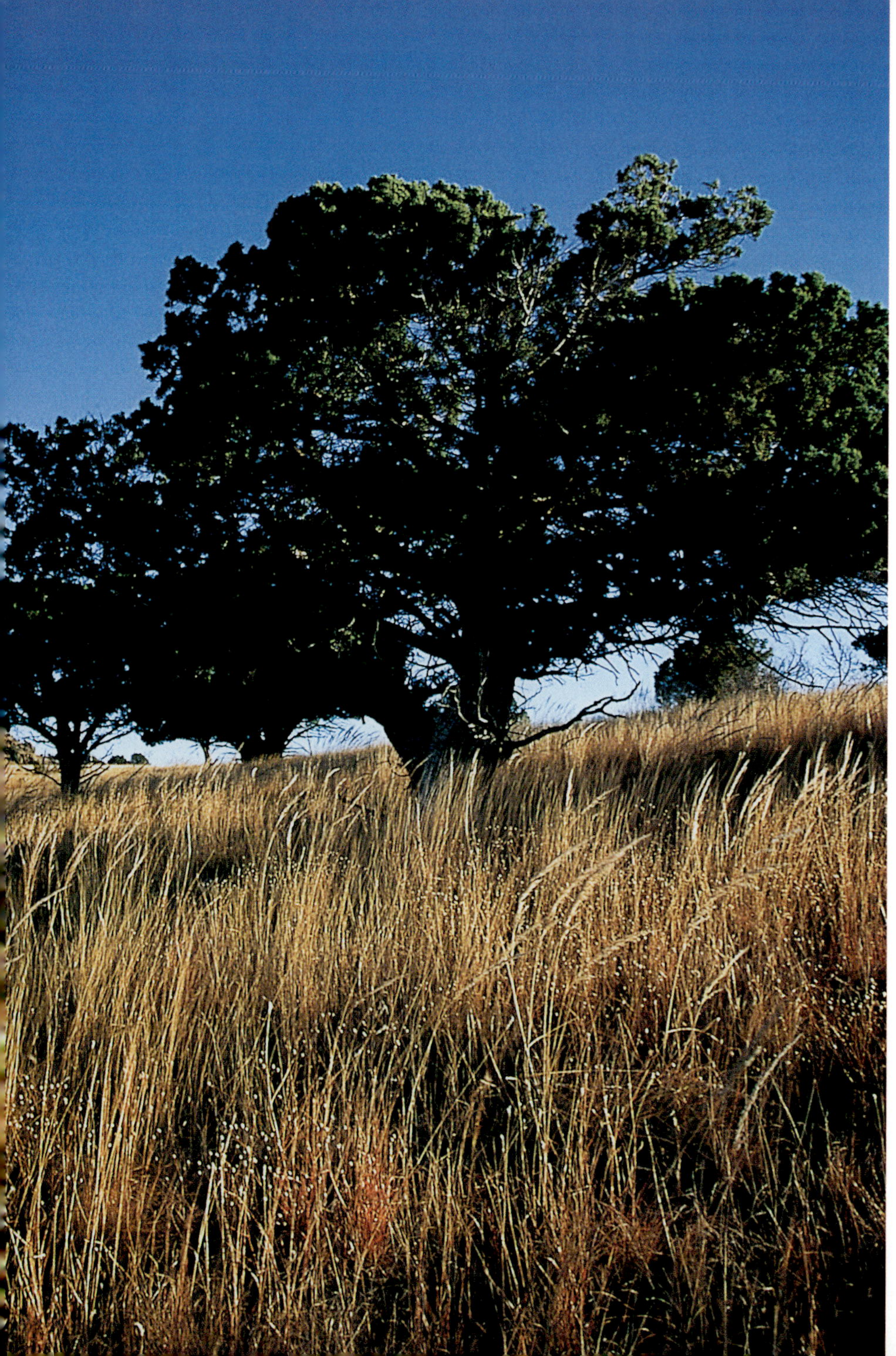

Alligator juniper savannah,
head of San Antonio Canyon,
morning

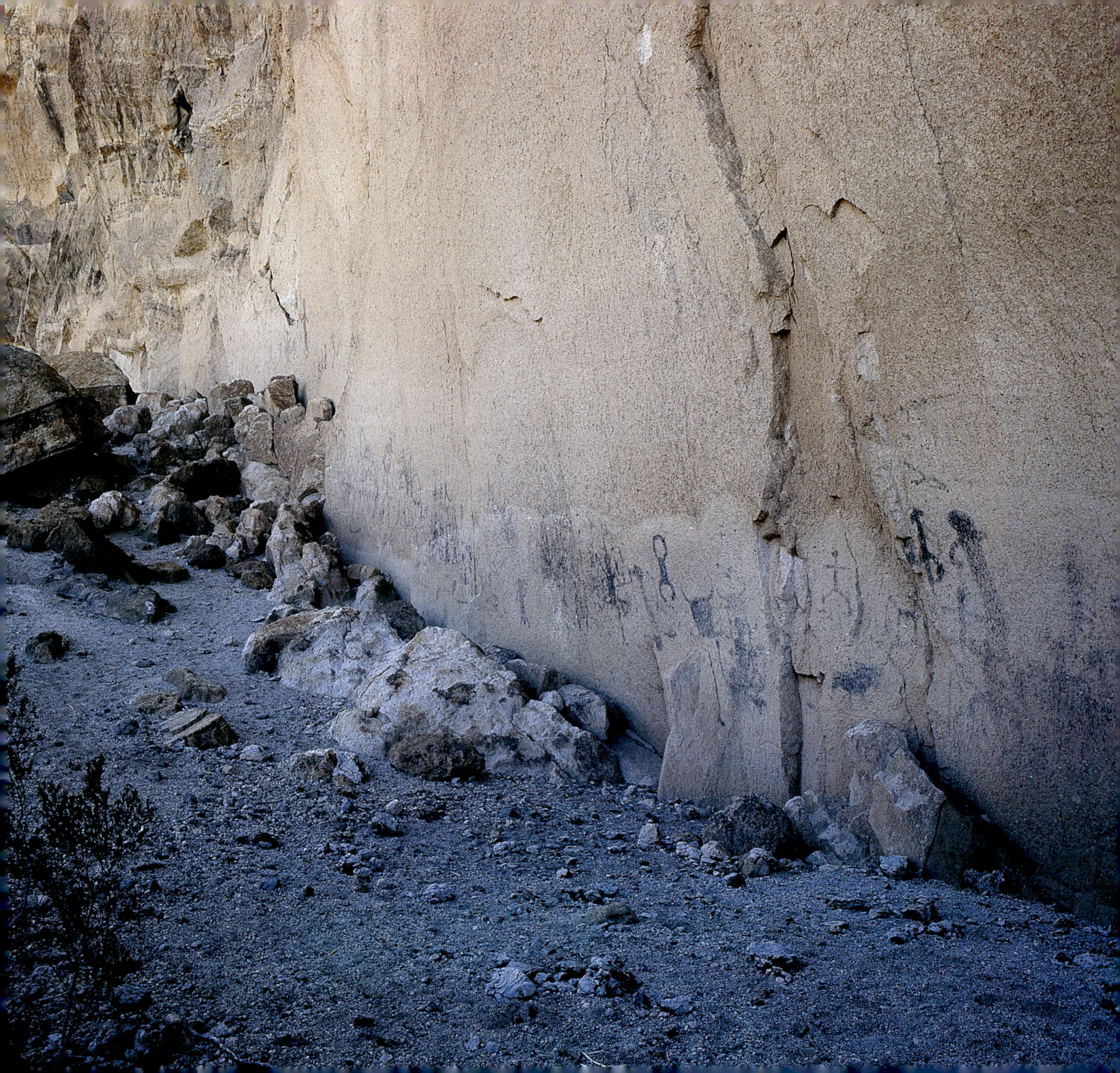

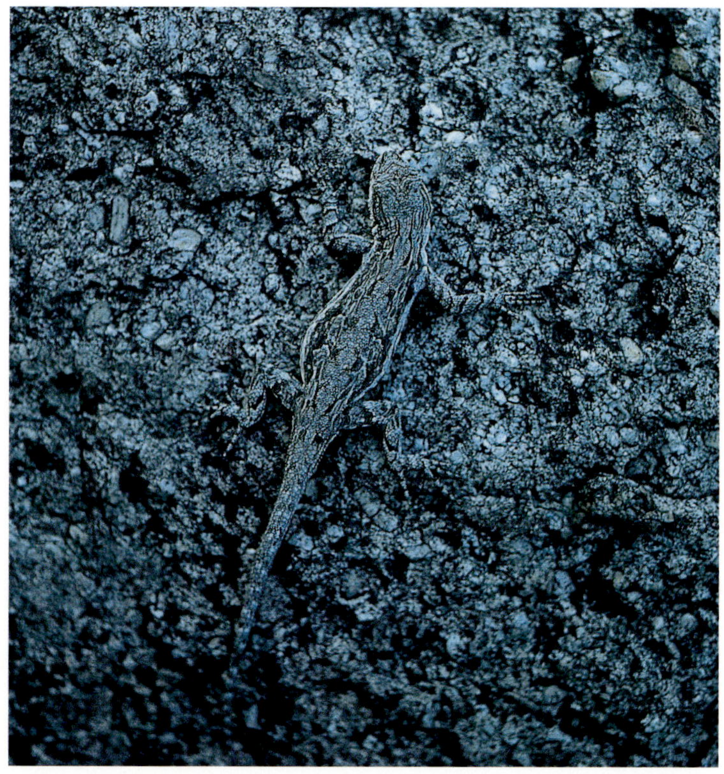

OPPOSITE: Rock art panel, Cuevas Amarillas, midday

ABOVE: Canyon lizard

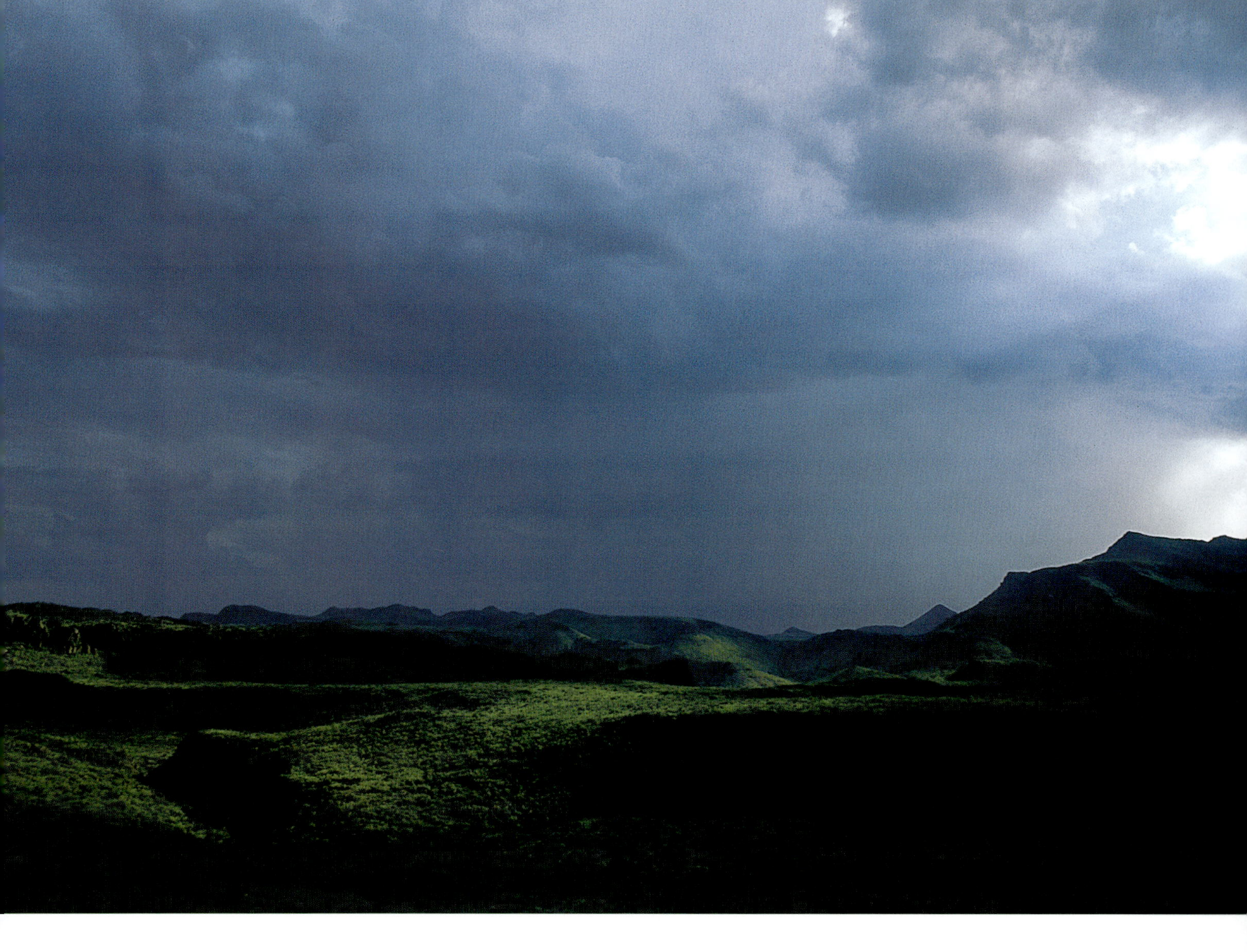

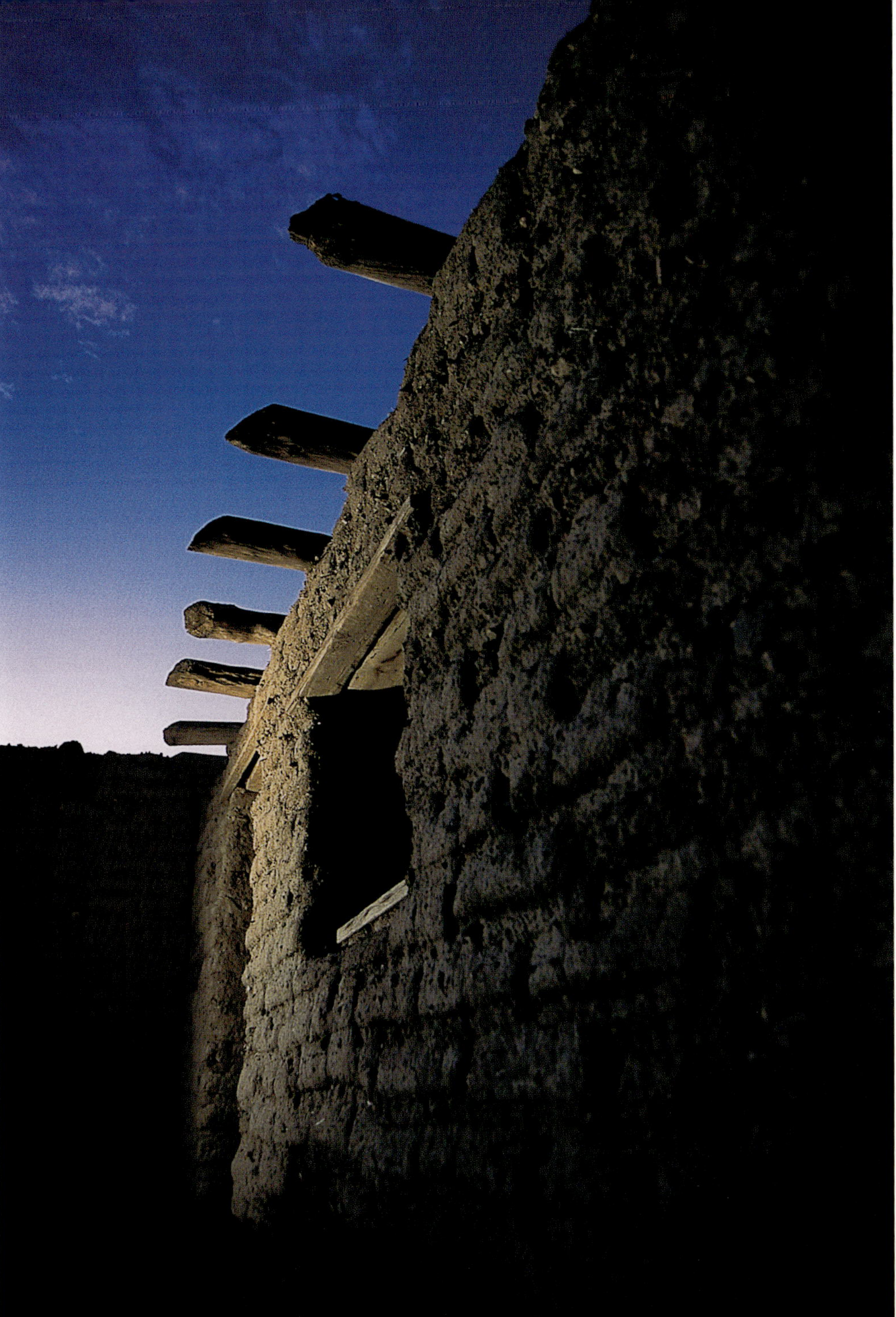

OPPOSITE: Summer monsoon, western edge of Big Bend Ranch, looking southwest, late afternoon

Madrid House, Madrid Canyon, twilight

Sunset over Oso Mountain

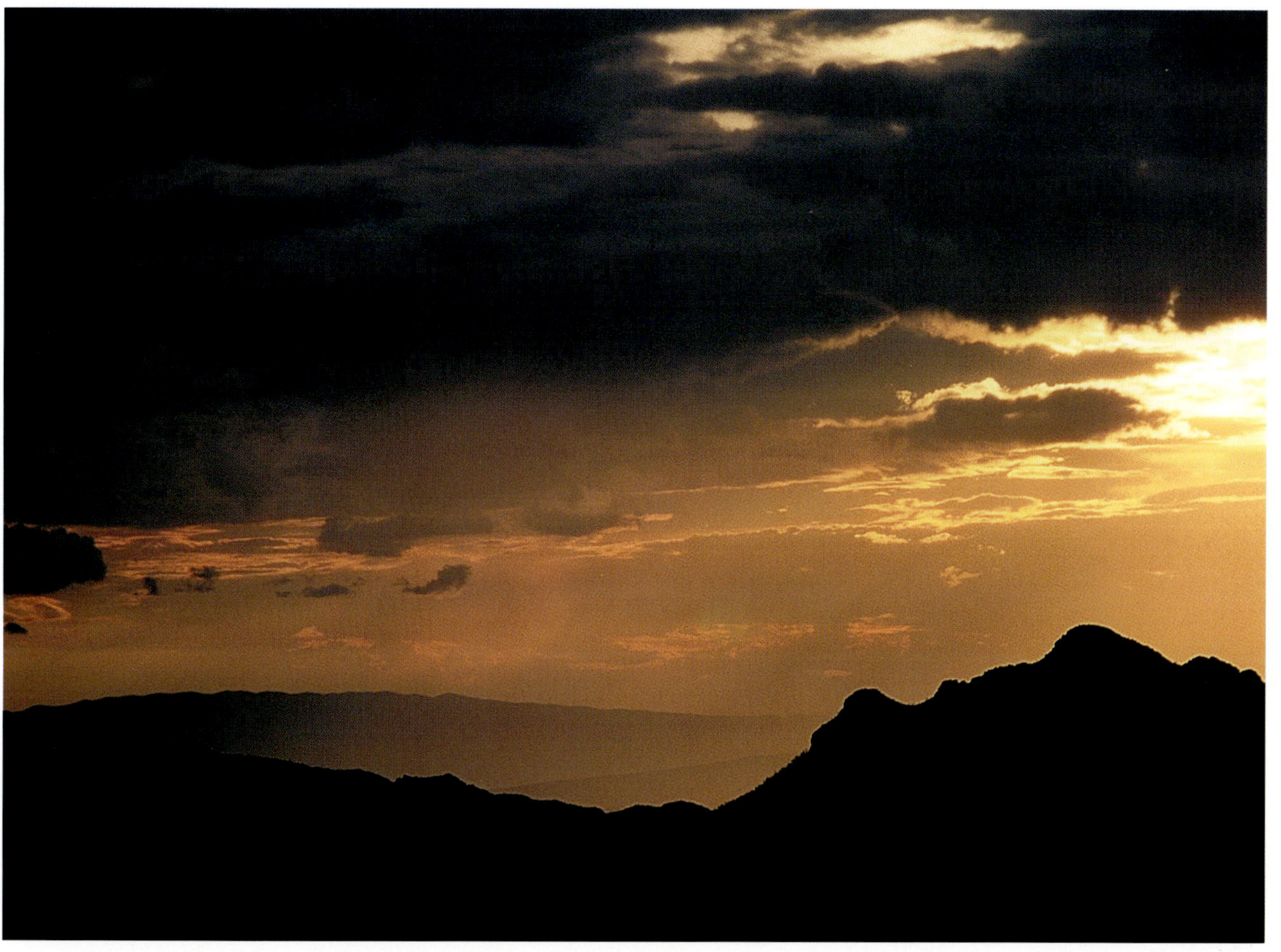

Sunset over western edge of Big Bend Ranch

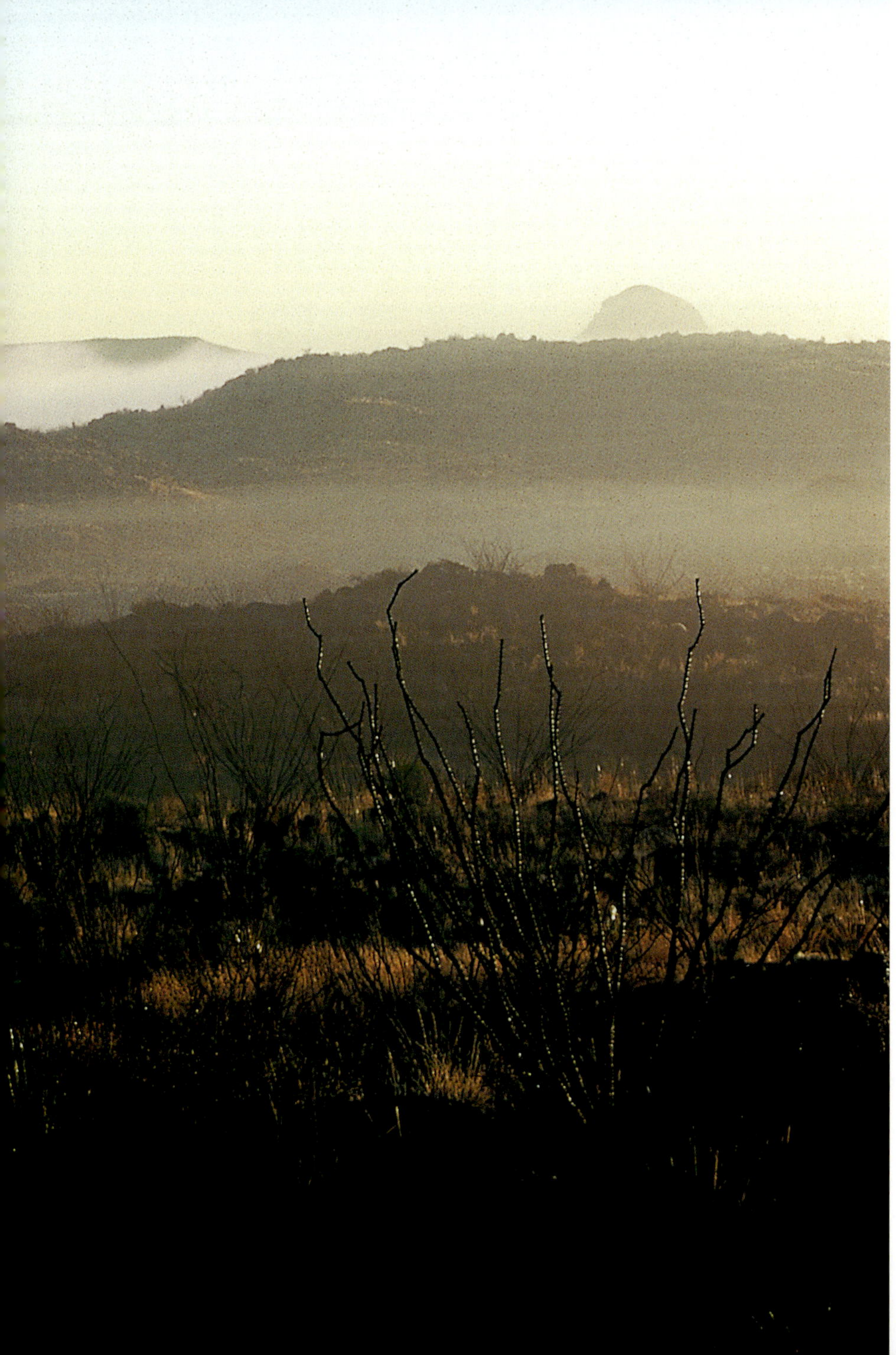

Desert fog, near Sauceda,
sunrise

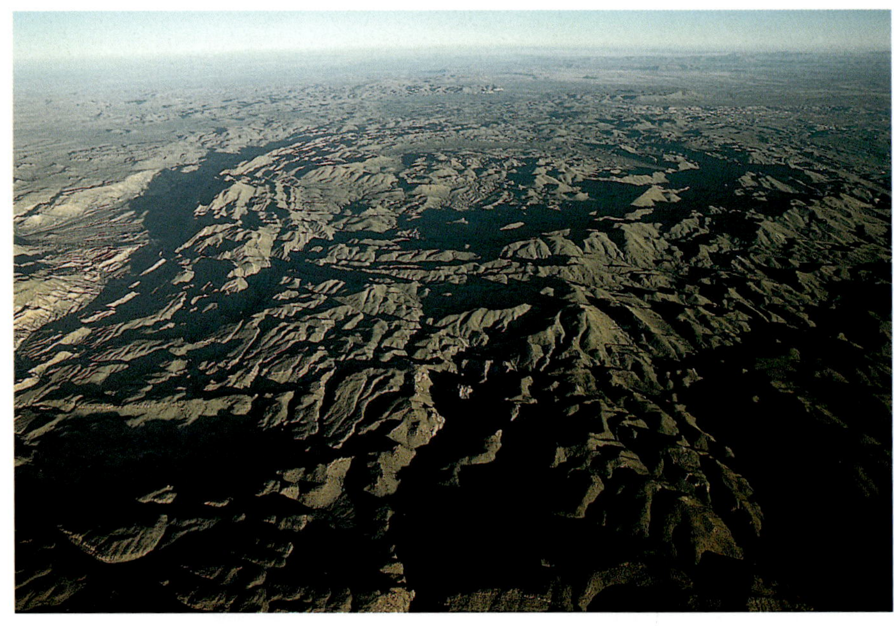

OPPOSITE: Sauceda, aerial view at sunrise; backdrop La Mota

ABOVE: Solitario, aerial view from 12,000 feet MSL

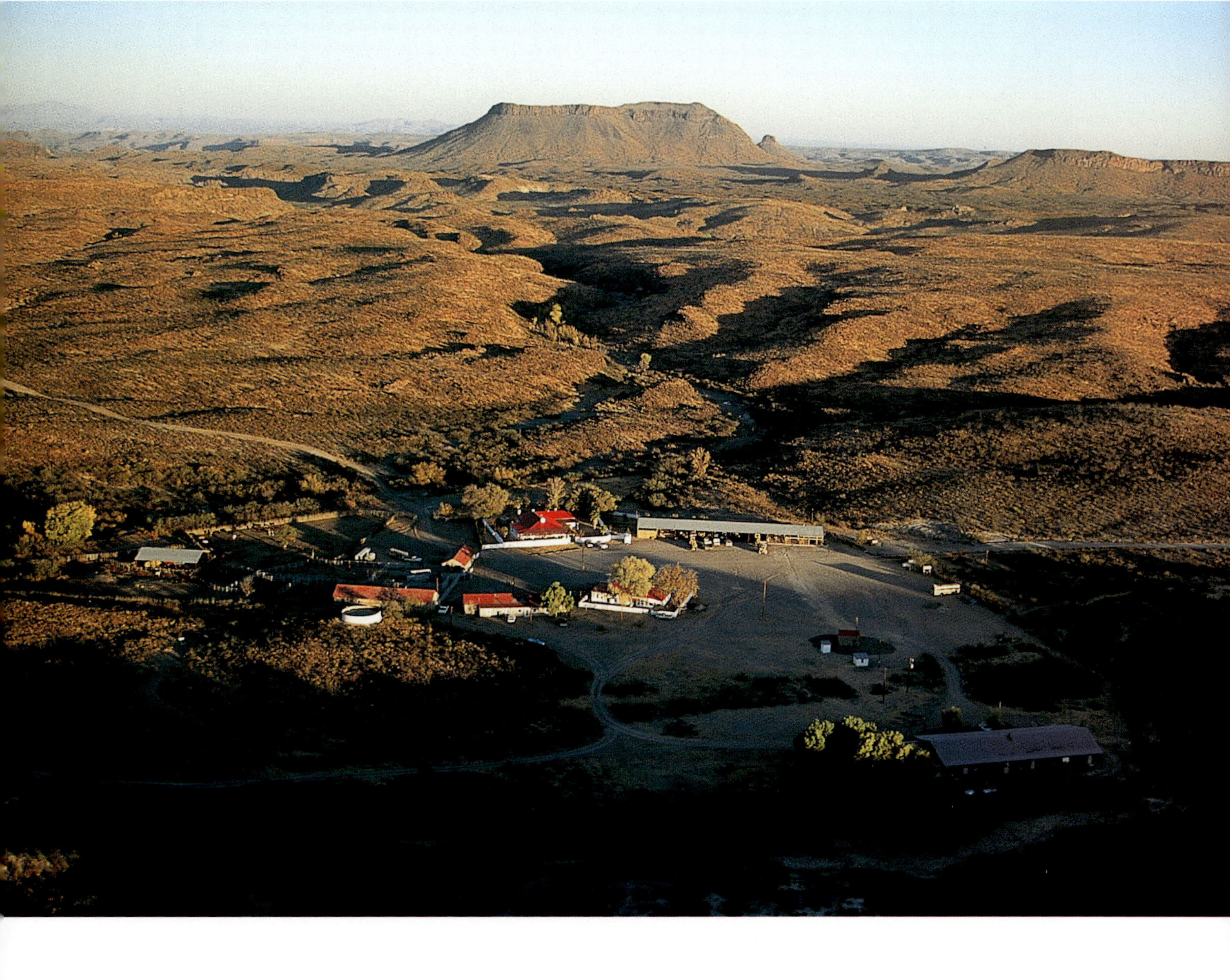

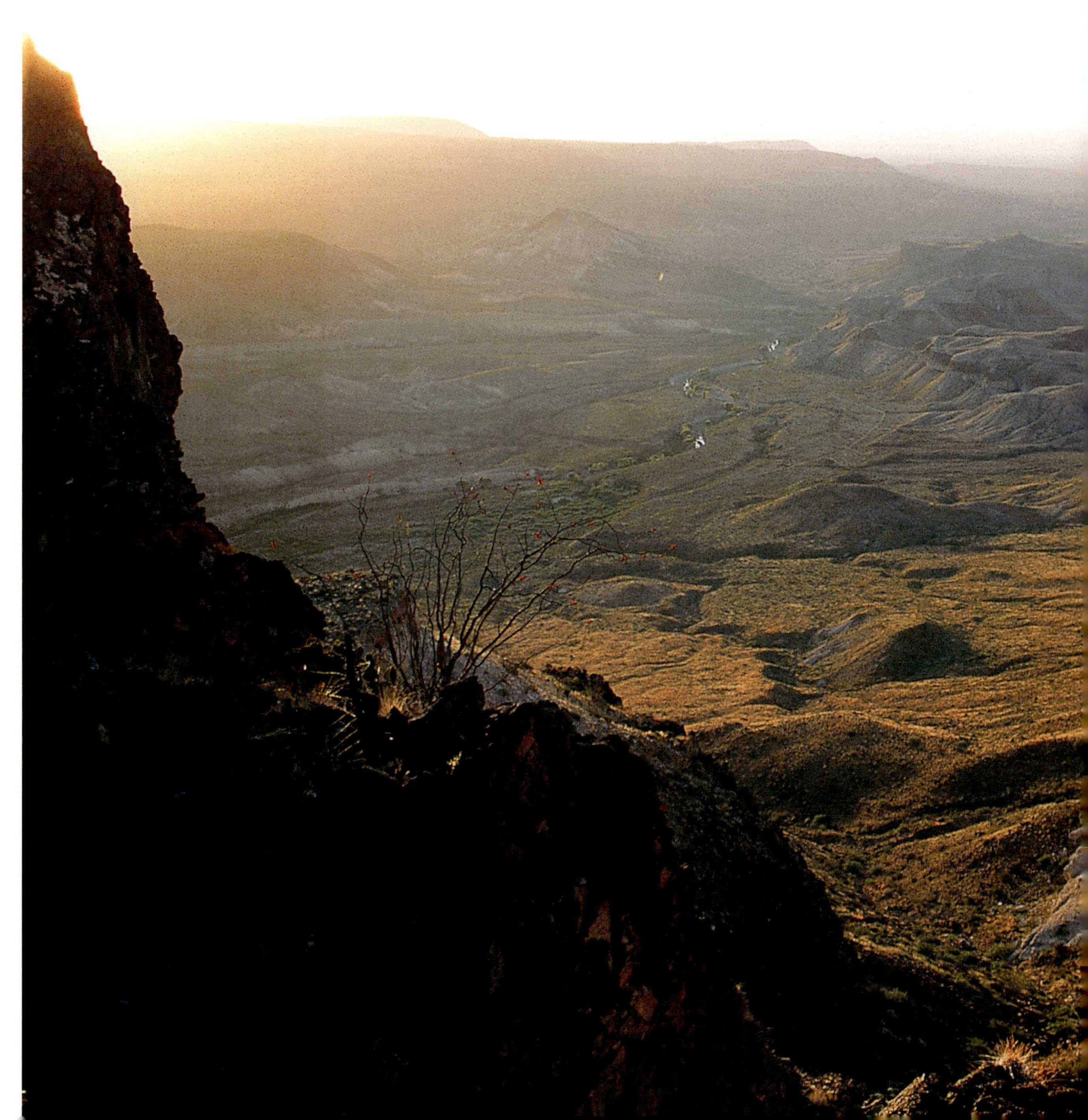

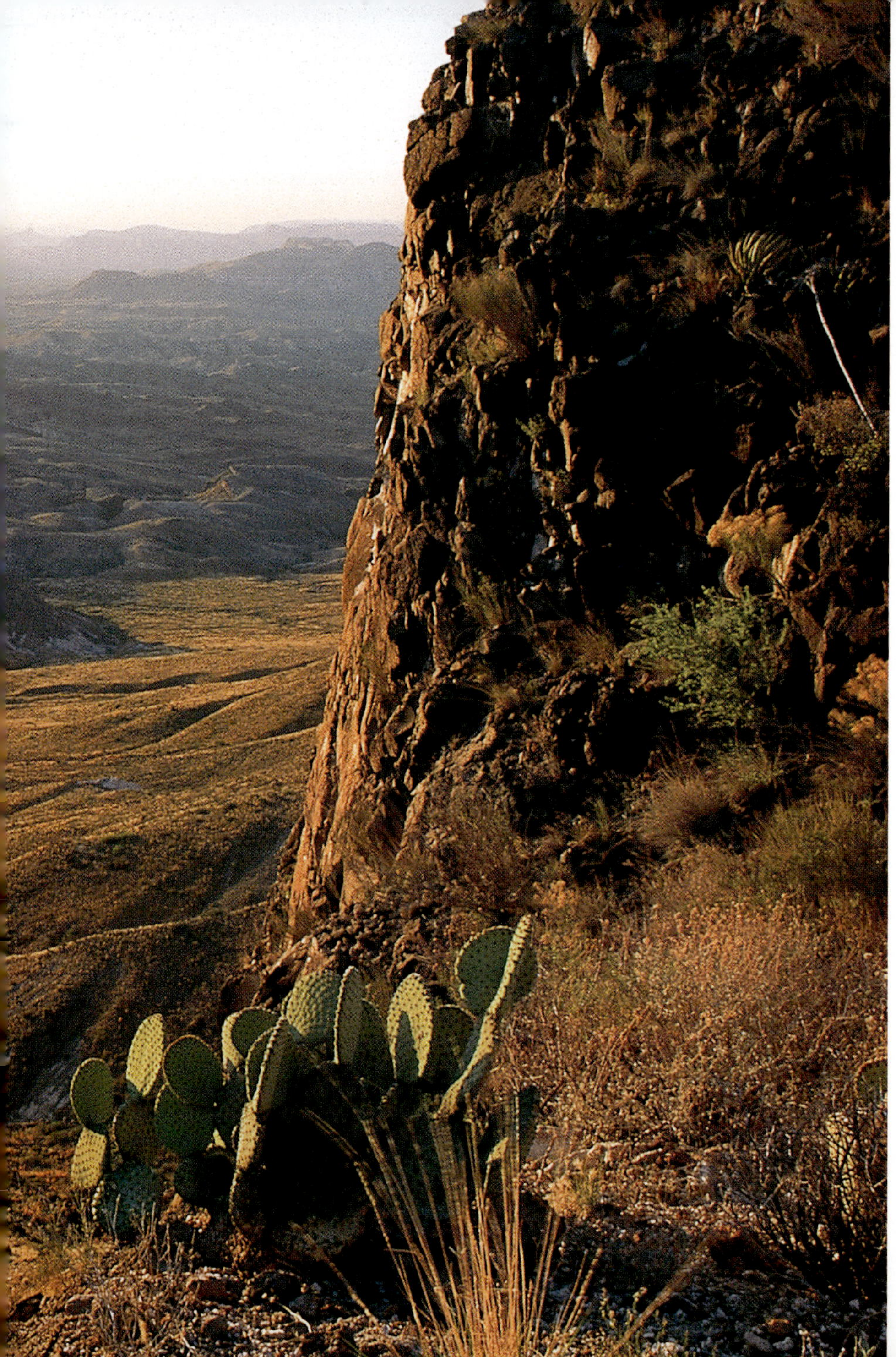

Sunrise over Fresno Canyon

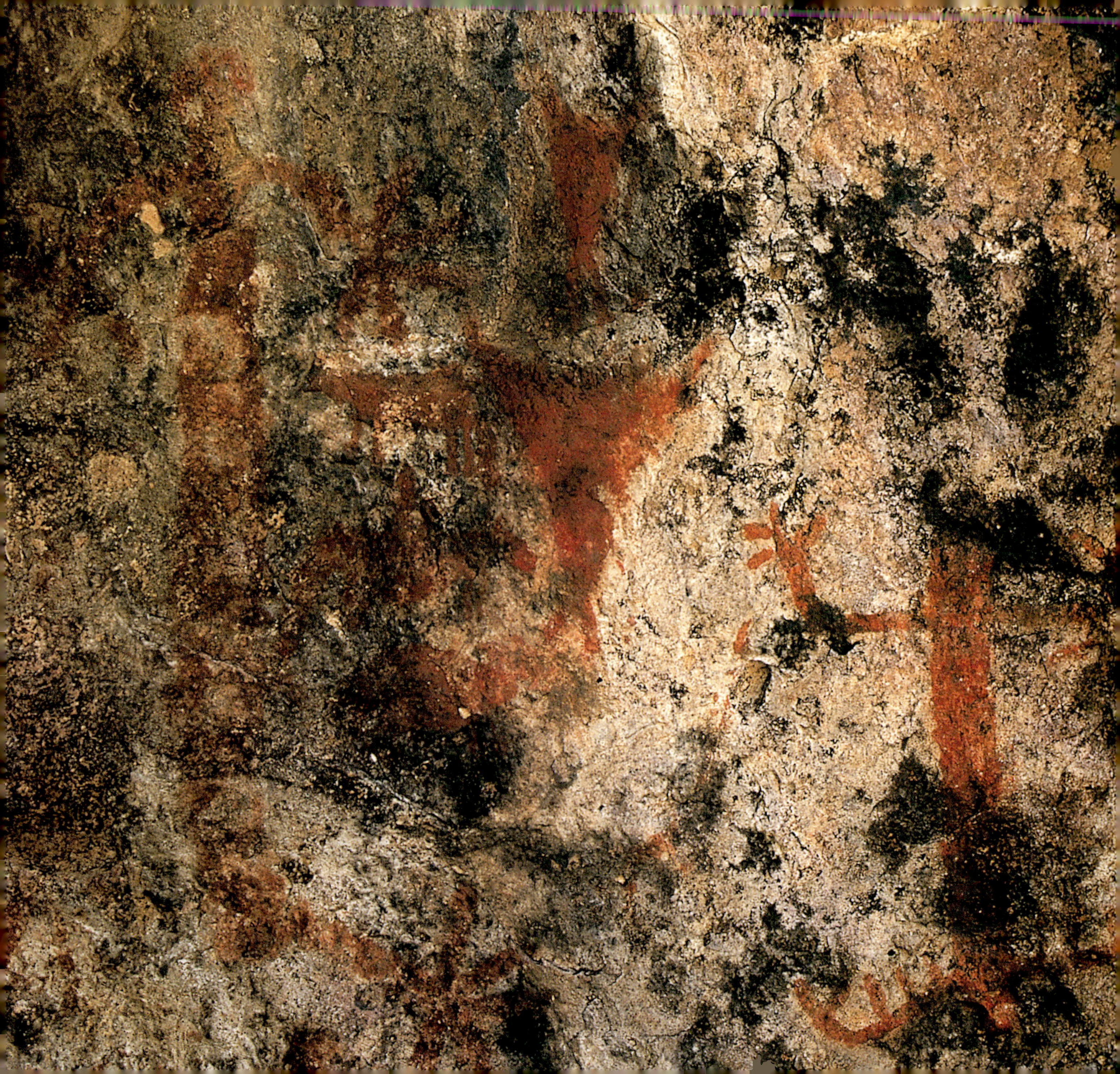

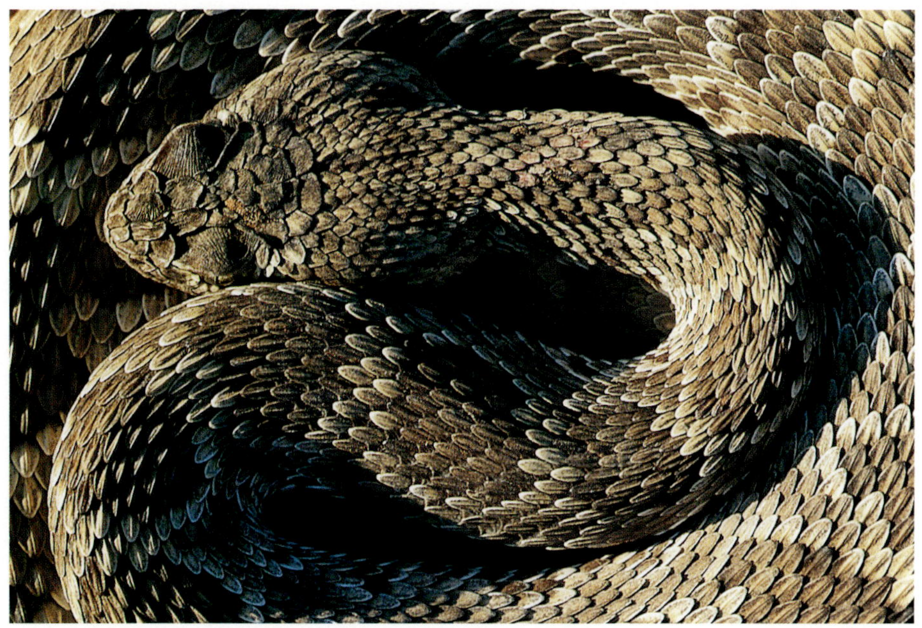

OPPOSITE: Rock art panel below Cinco Tinajas

ABOVE: Mojave rattlesnake

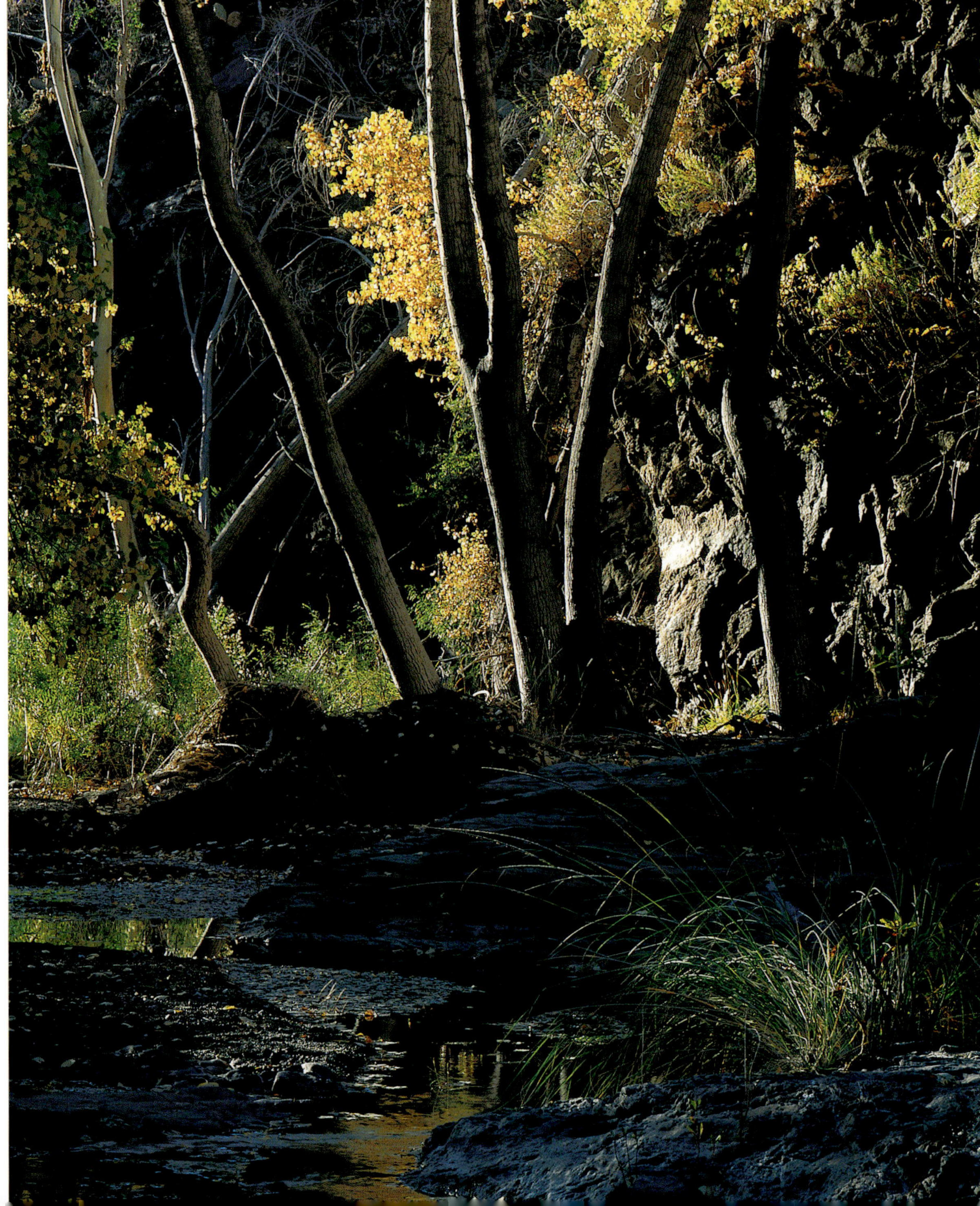

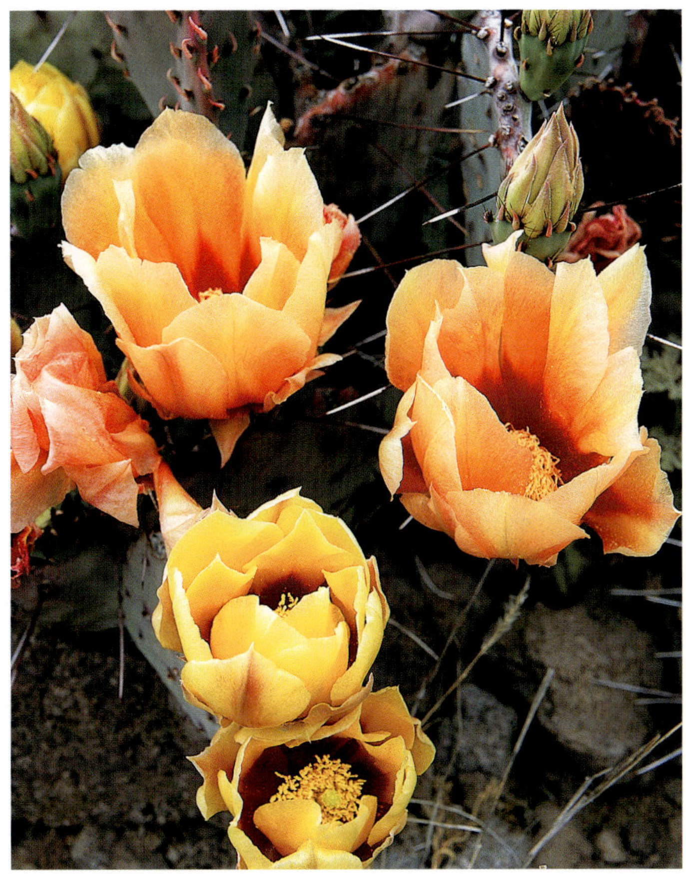

OPPOSITE: Cottonwoods in fall foliage, Arroyo Segundo, sunrise

ABOVE: Prickly pear blooms near Sauceda, morning

Bedrock mortar and autumn leaves, Segundo Arroyo, morning

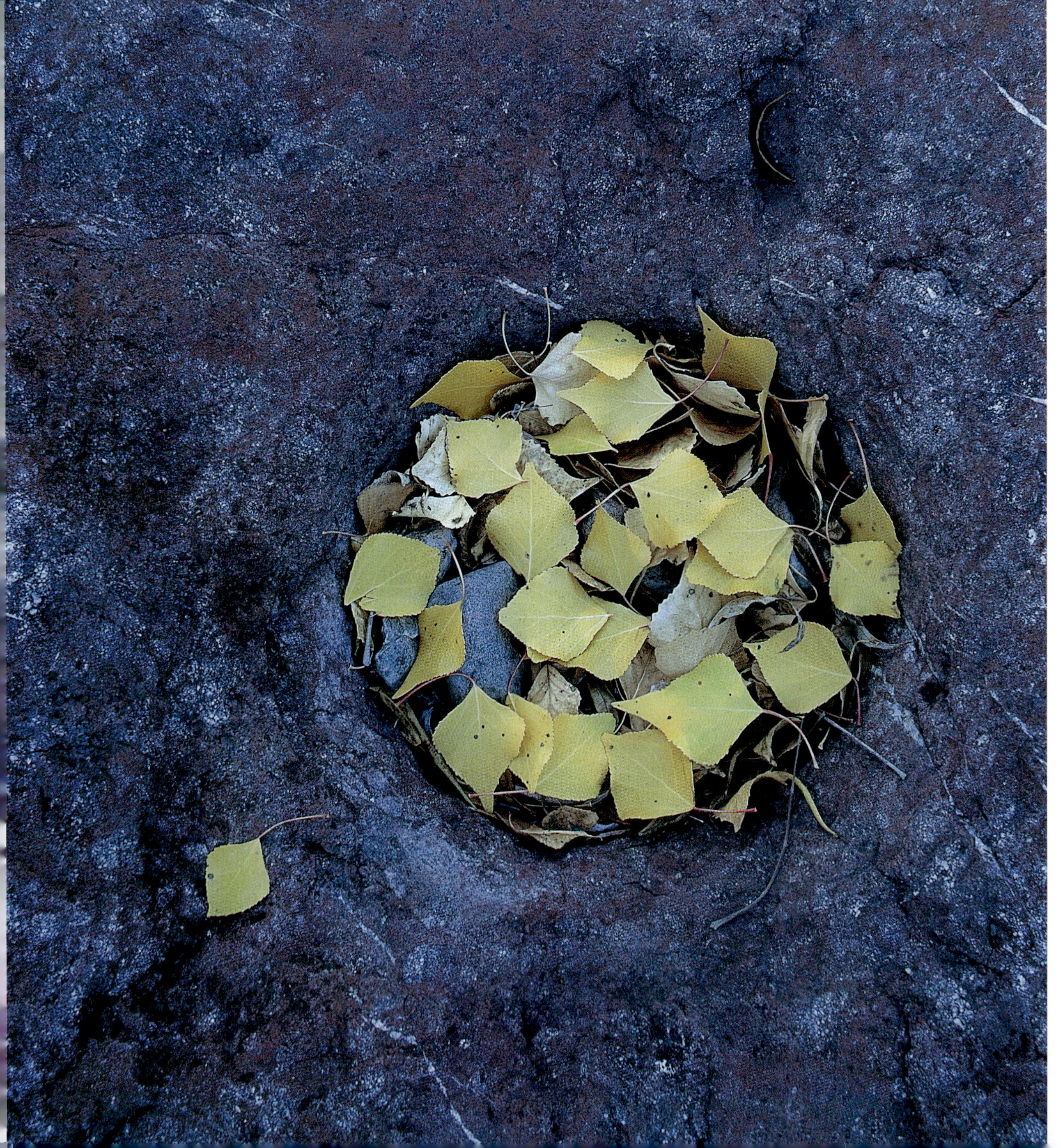

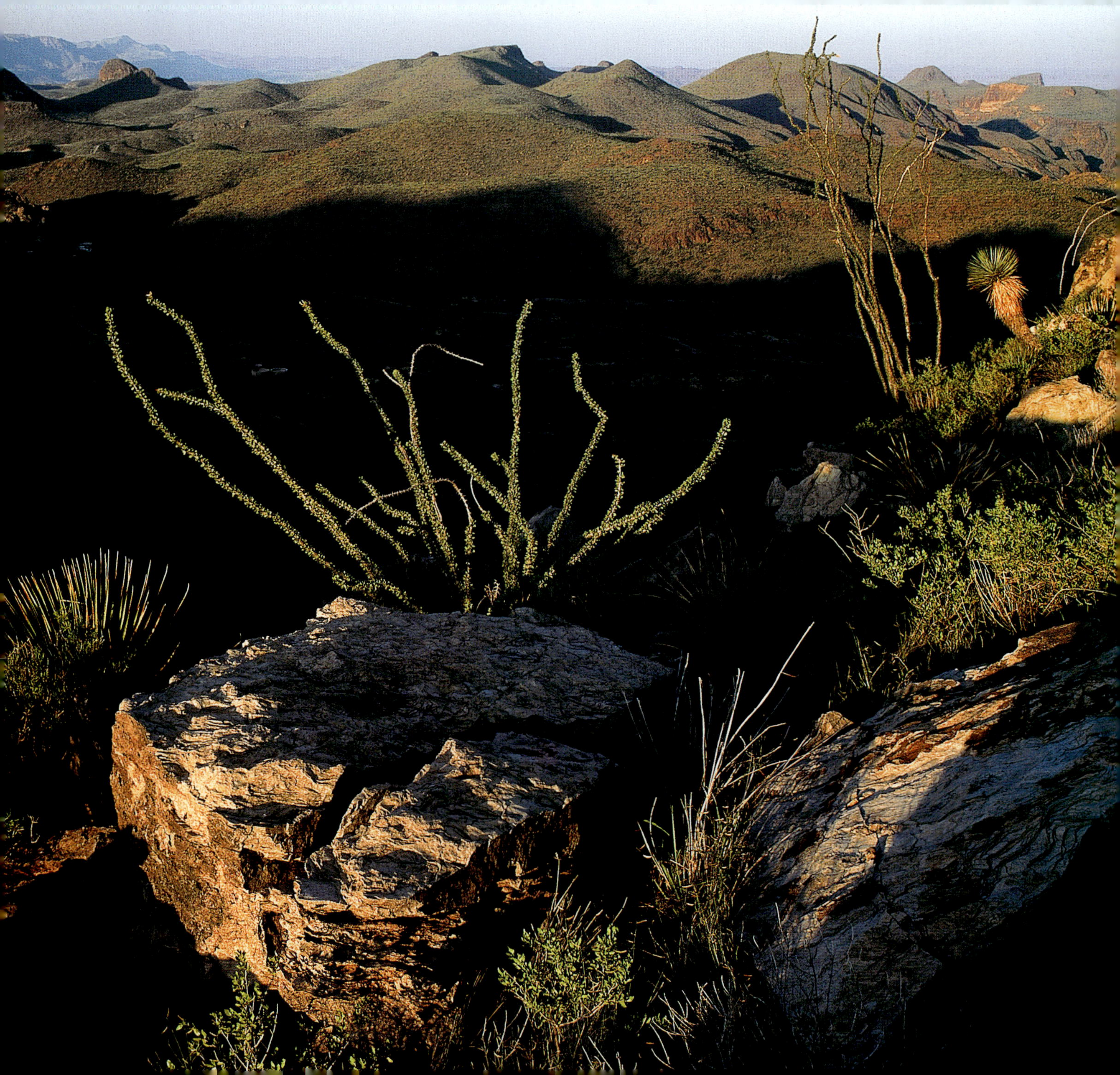

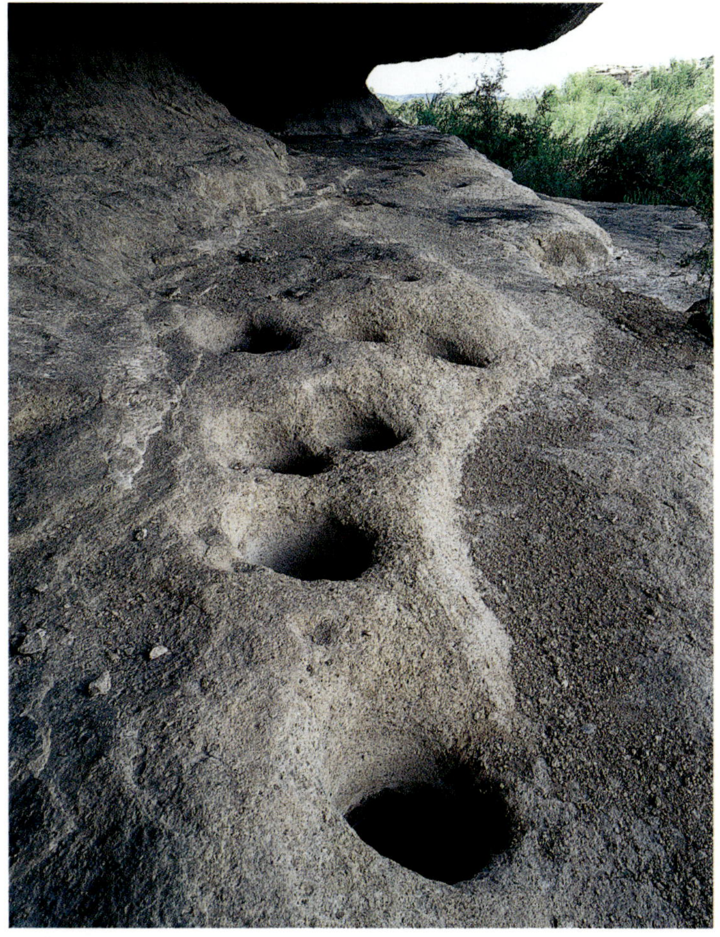

OPPOSITE: Southeast of Oso Mountain, looking southwest, sunrise

ABOVE: Bedrock mortars in Las Cuevas, western edge of Big Bend Ranch, morning

Boulder ridge, southwest of Sauceda, looking southeast, sunrise

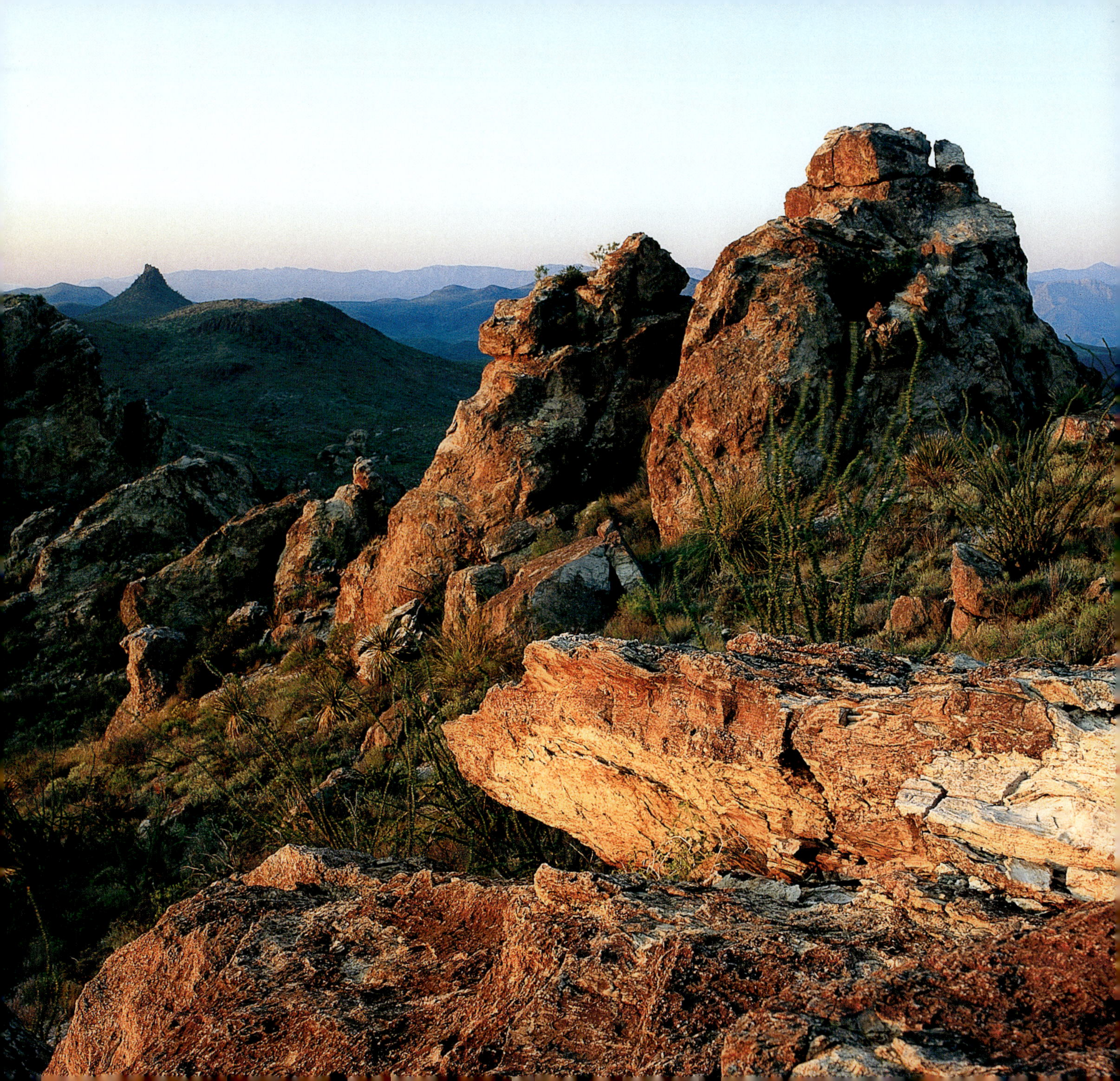

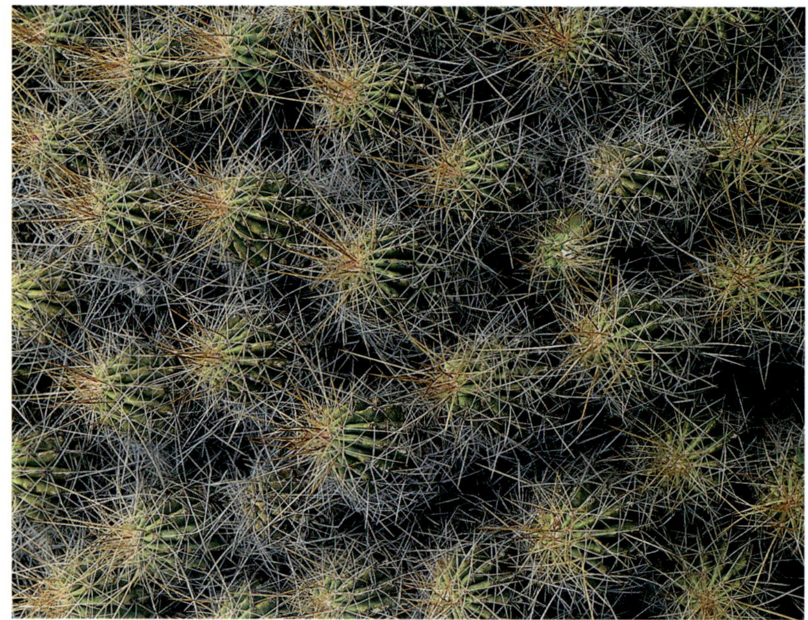

OPPOSITE: Monsoon season on the Big Bend Ranch, October

ABOVE: Hedgehog cactus, near Fresno Canyon

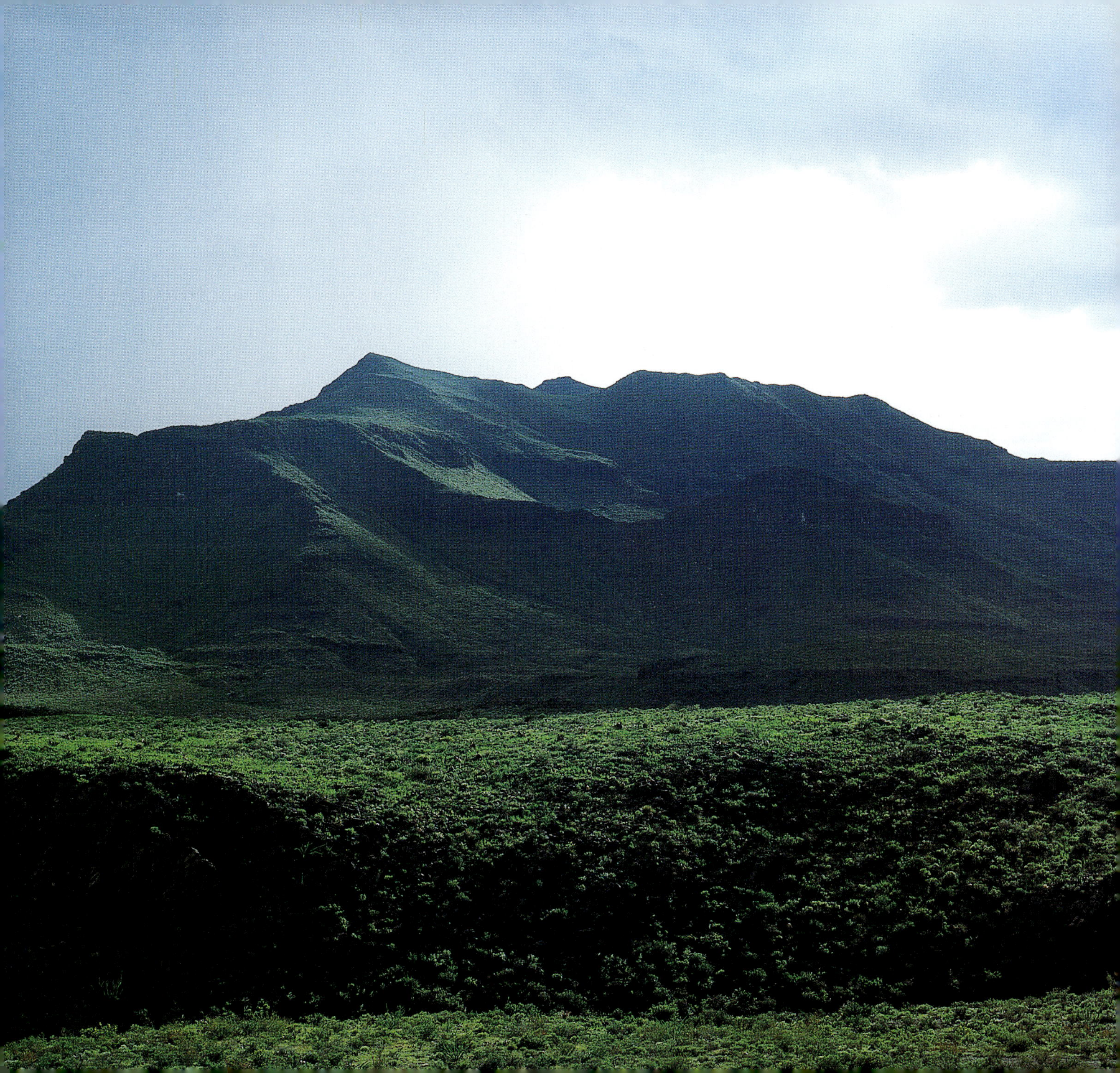

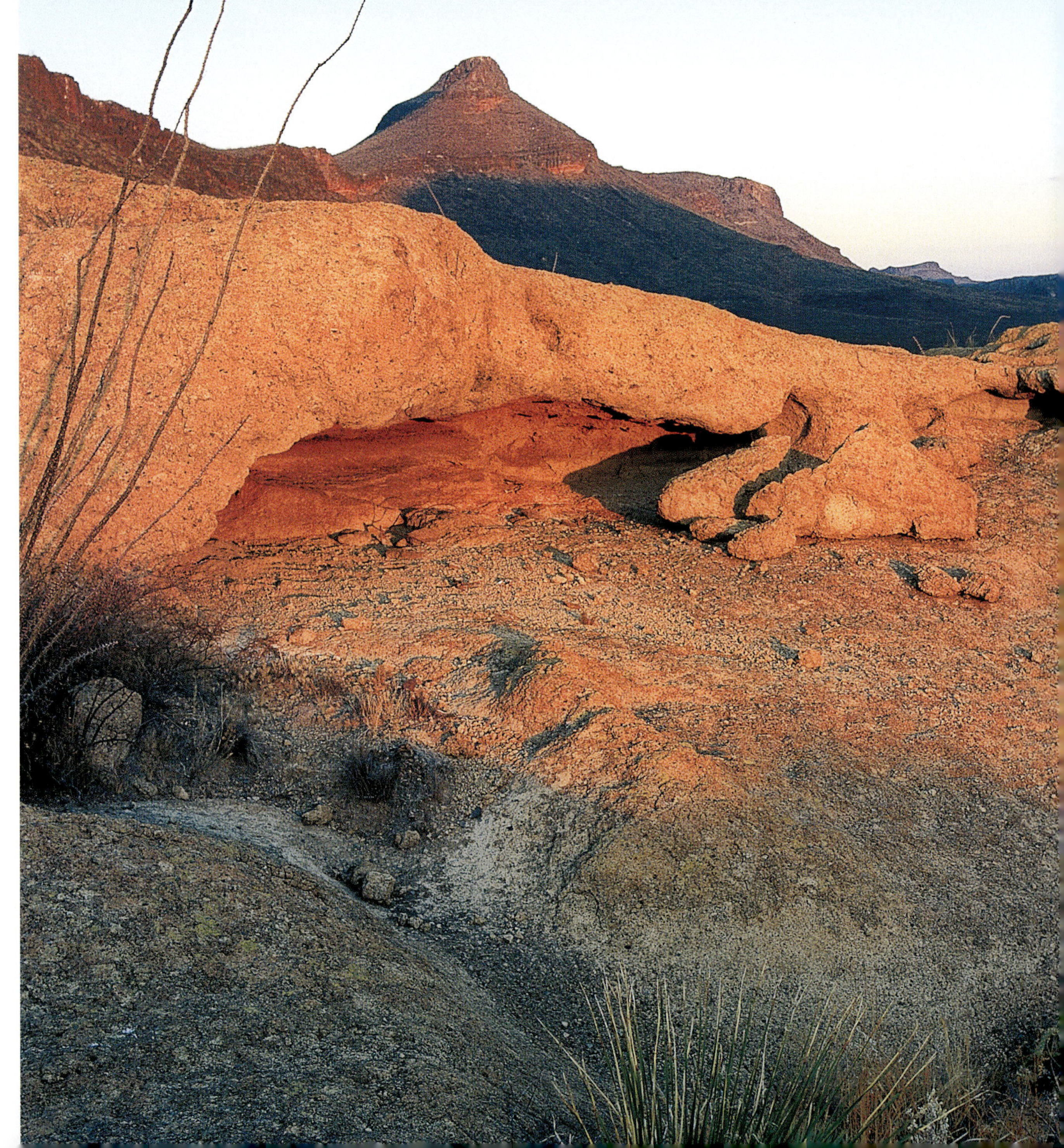

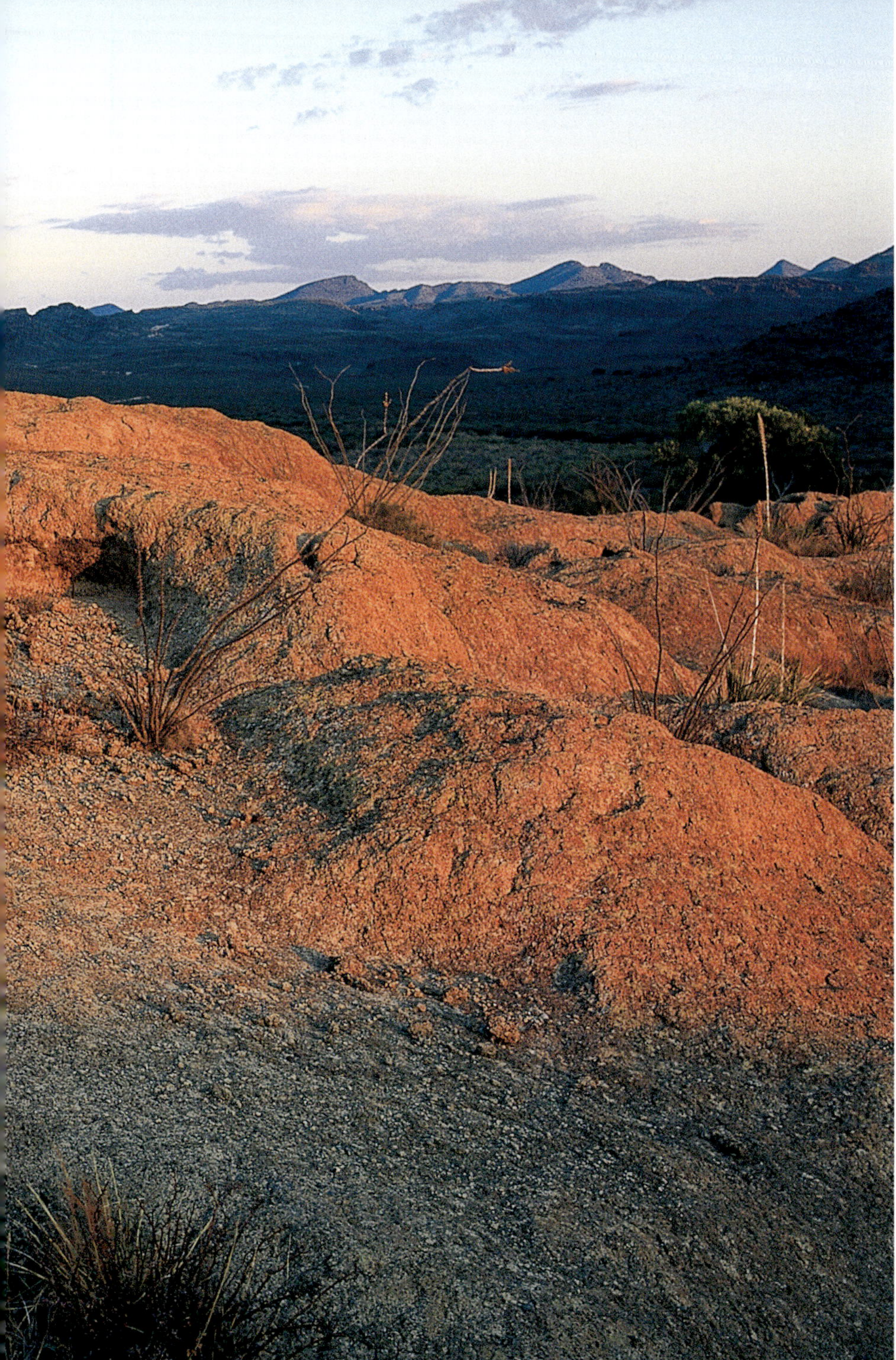

Rock shelter, Los Cuevas, sunset

Eastern rim of Fresno Canyon,
looking south, late afternoon

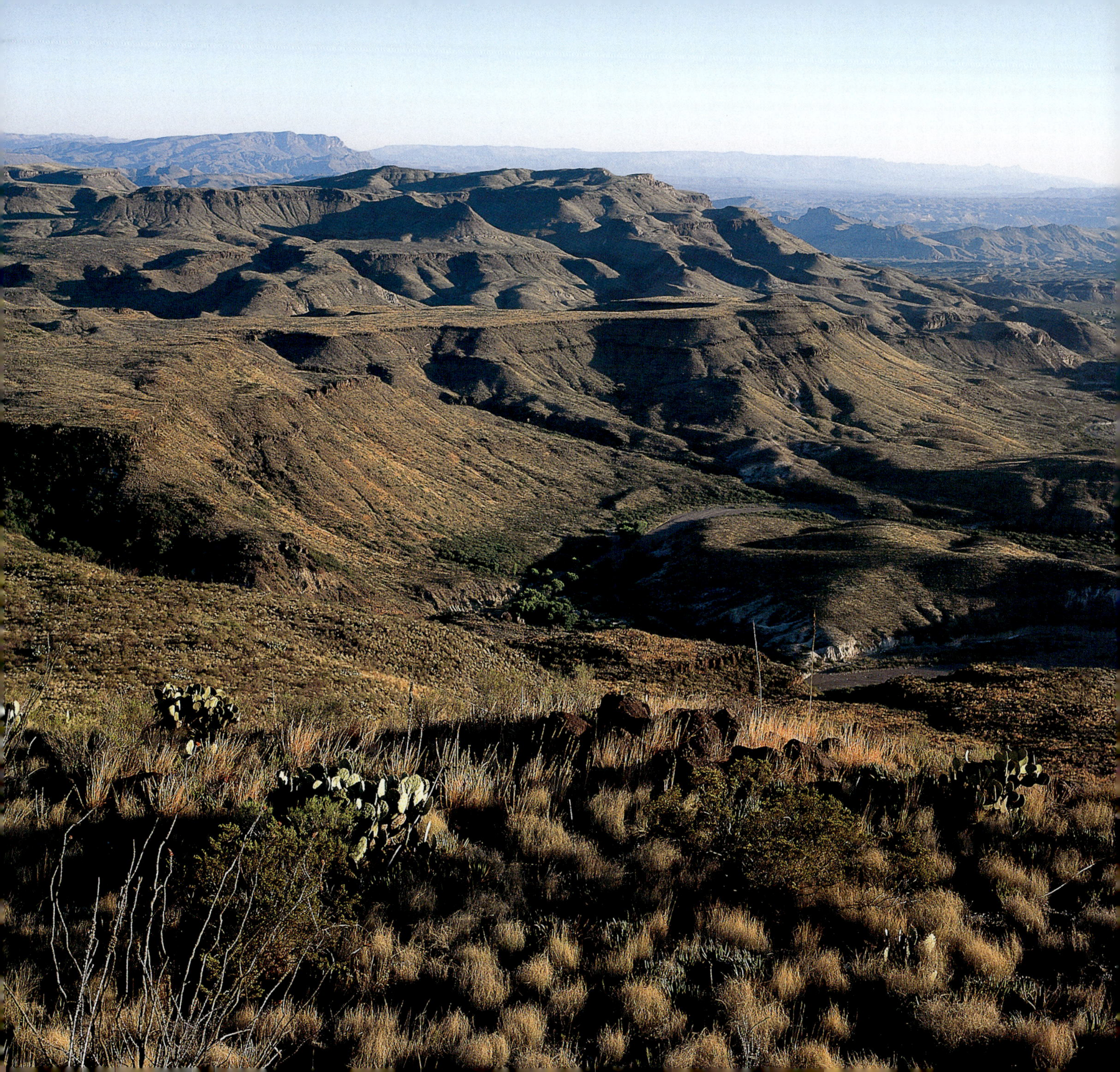

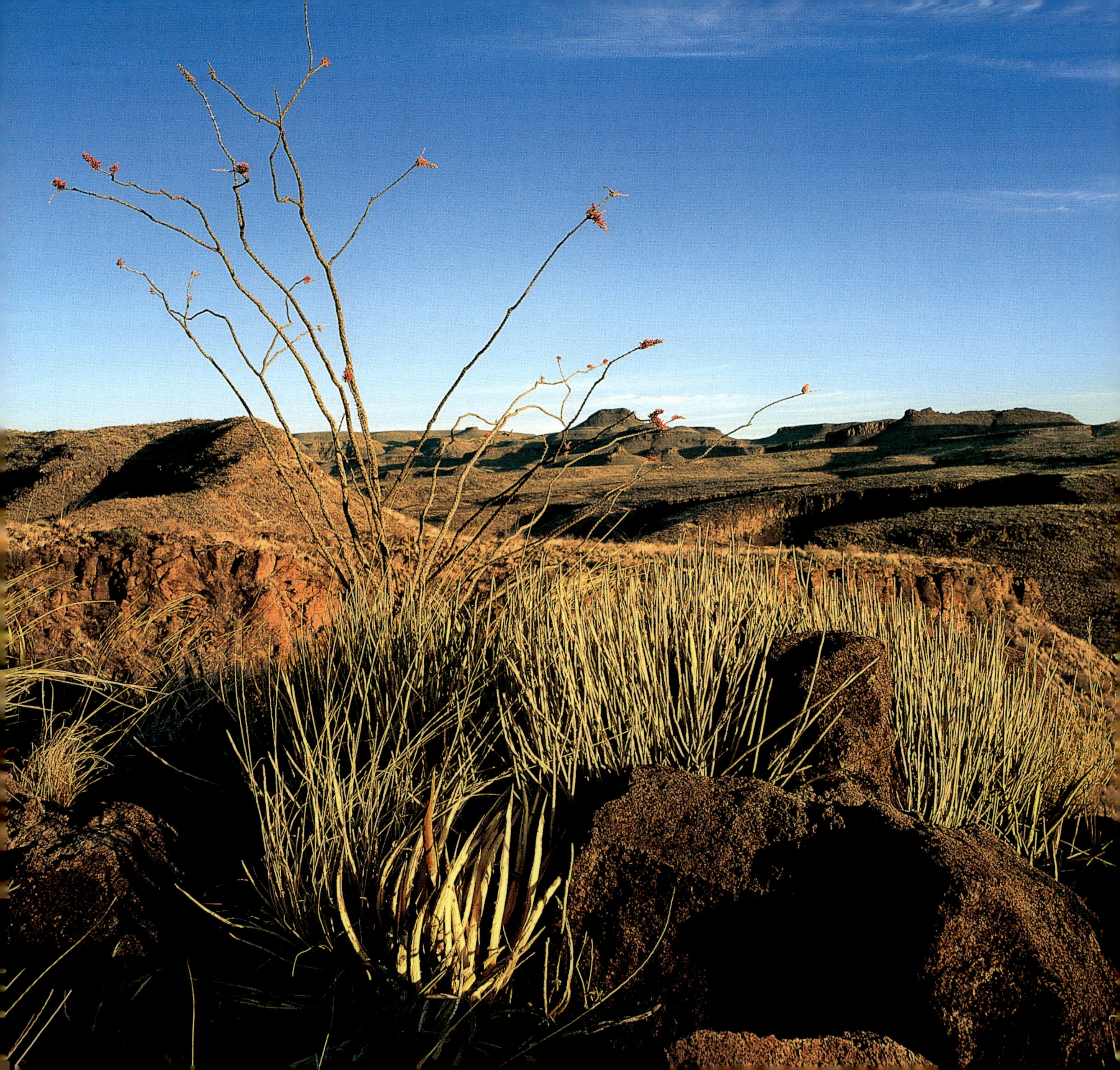

Candelilla and ocotillo, near
Madrid Falls, late afternoon

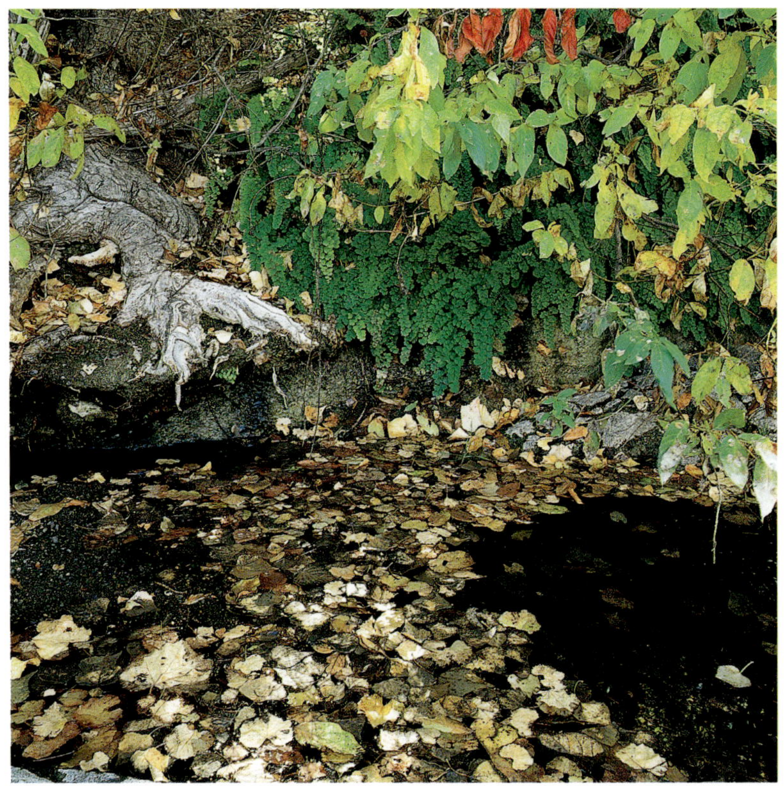

OPPOSITE: Big Bend bluebonnets, near Cinco Tinajas, midday

ABOVE: Springwater and fall foliage, Madrid Canyon, midday

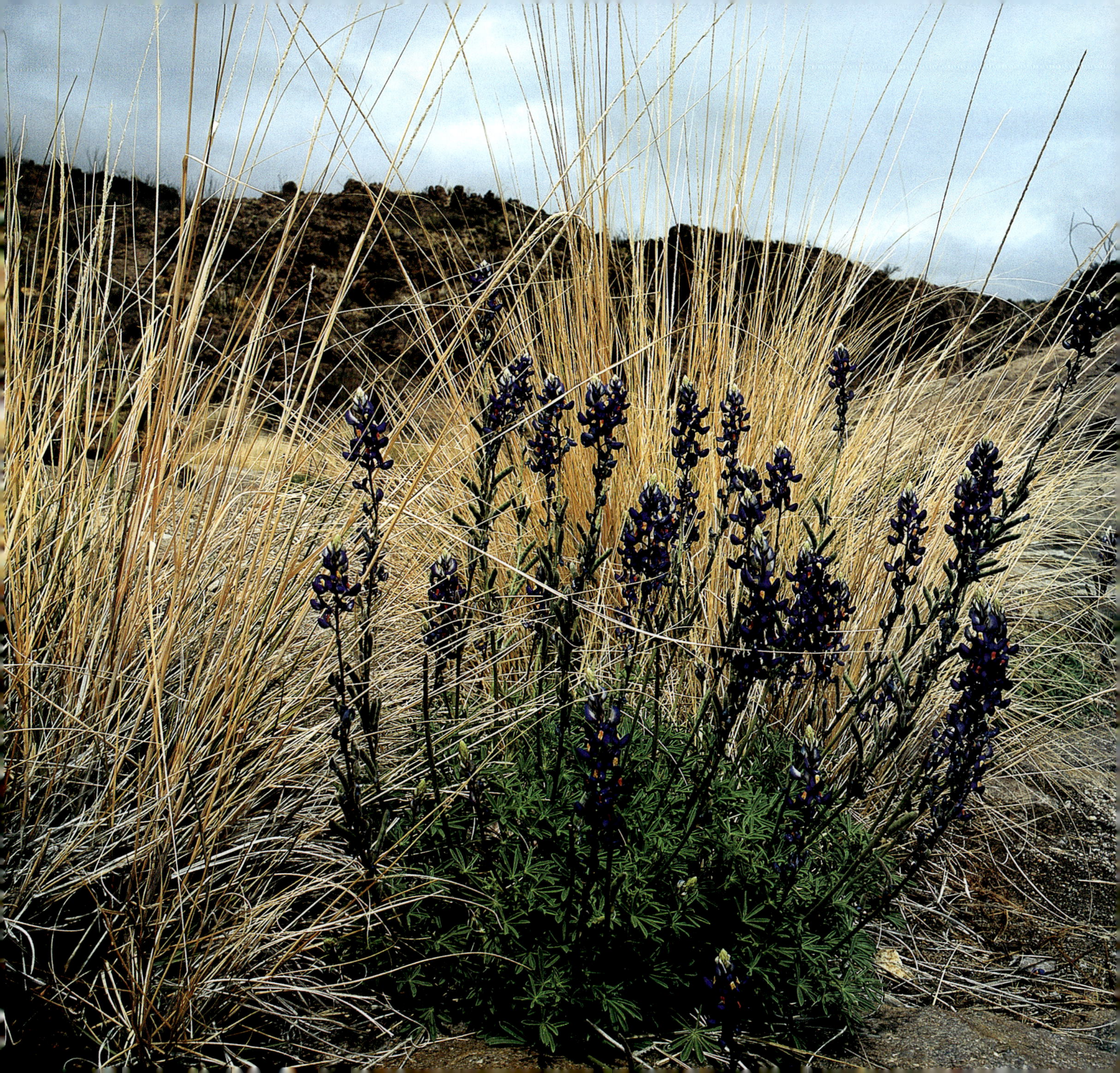

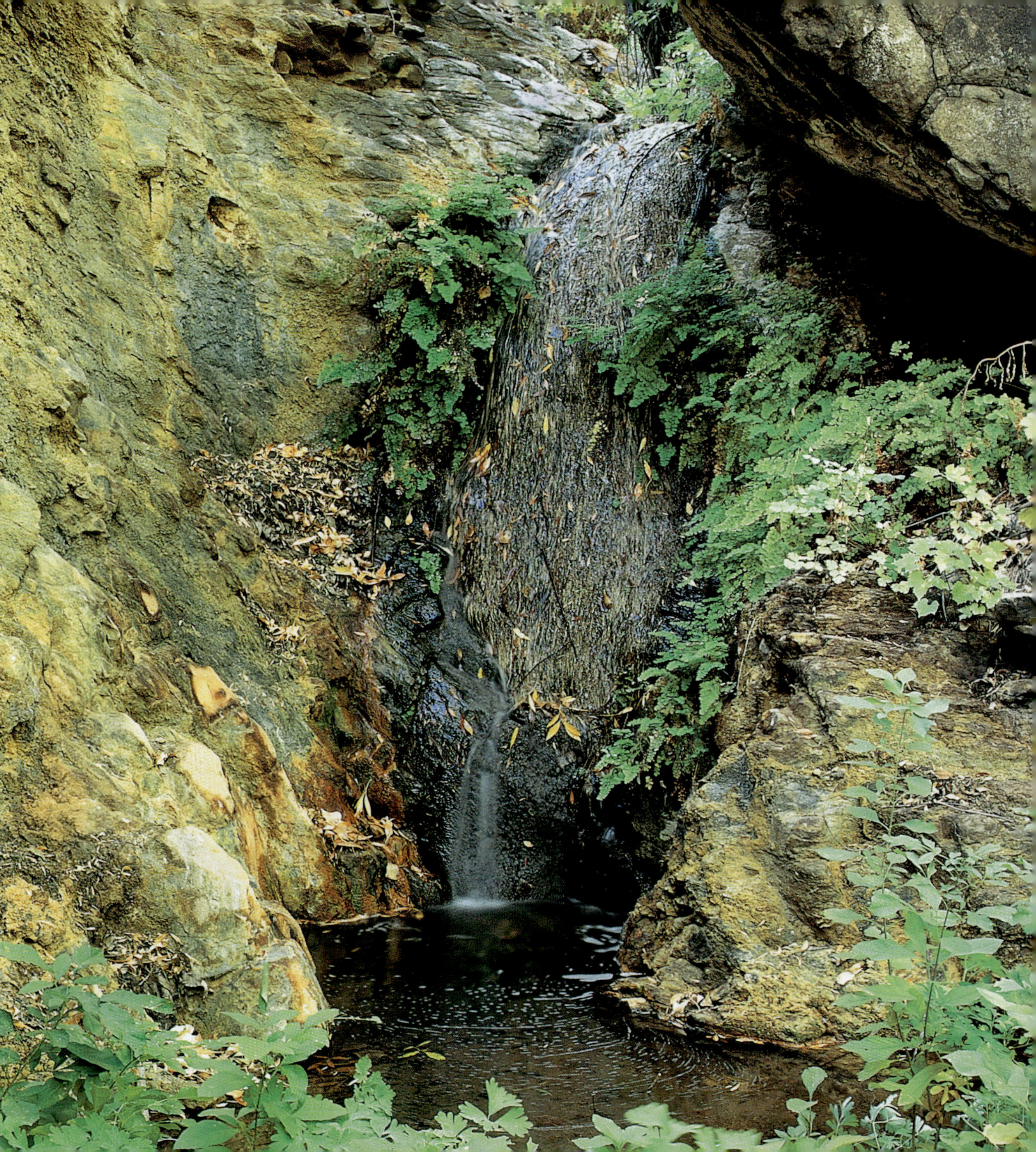

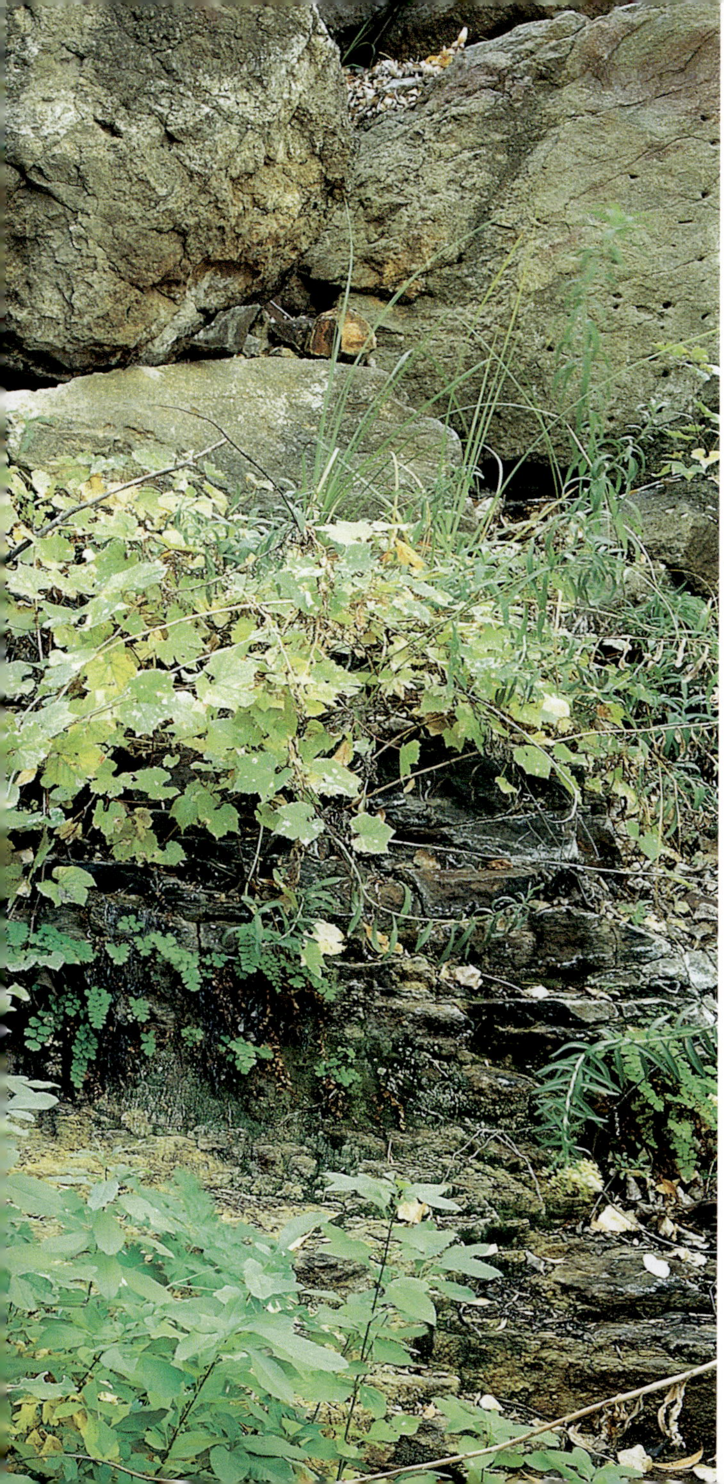

Spring Canyon, tributary to Fresno, midday

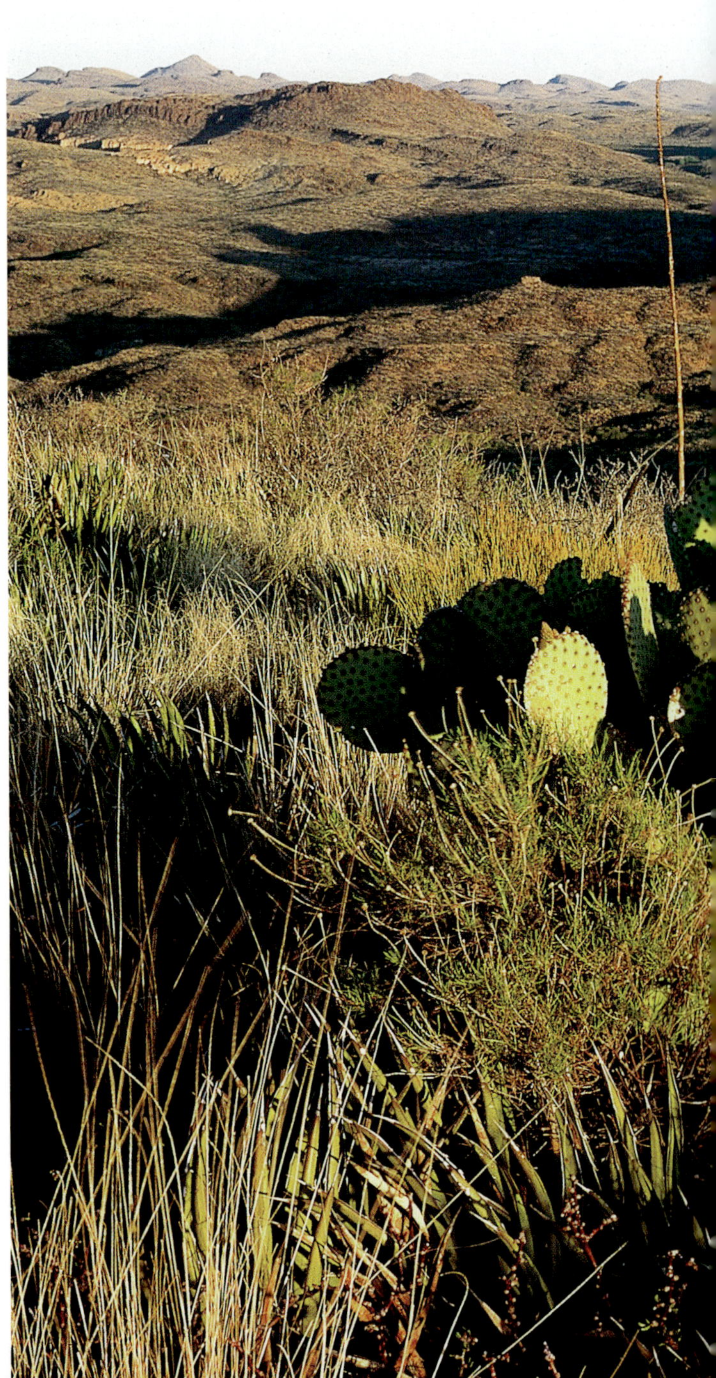

Lechuguilla and prickly pear, looking west toward Guitar Mountain, early morning

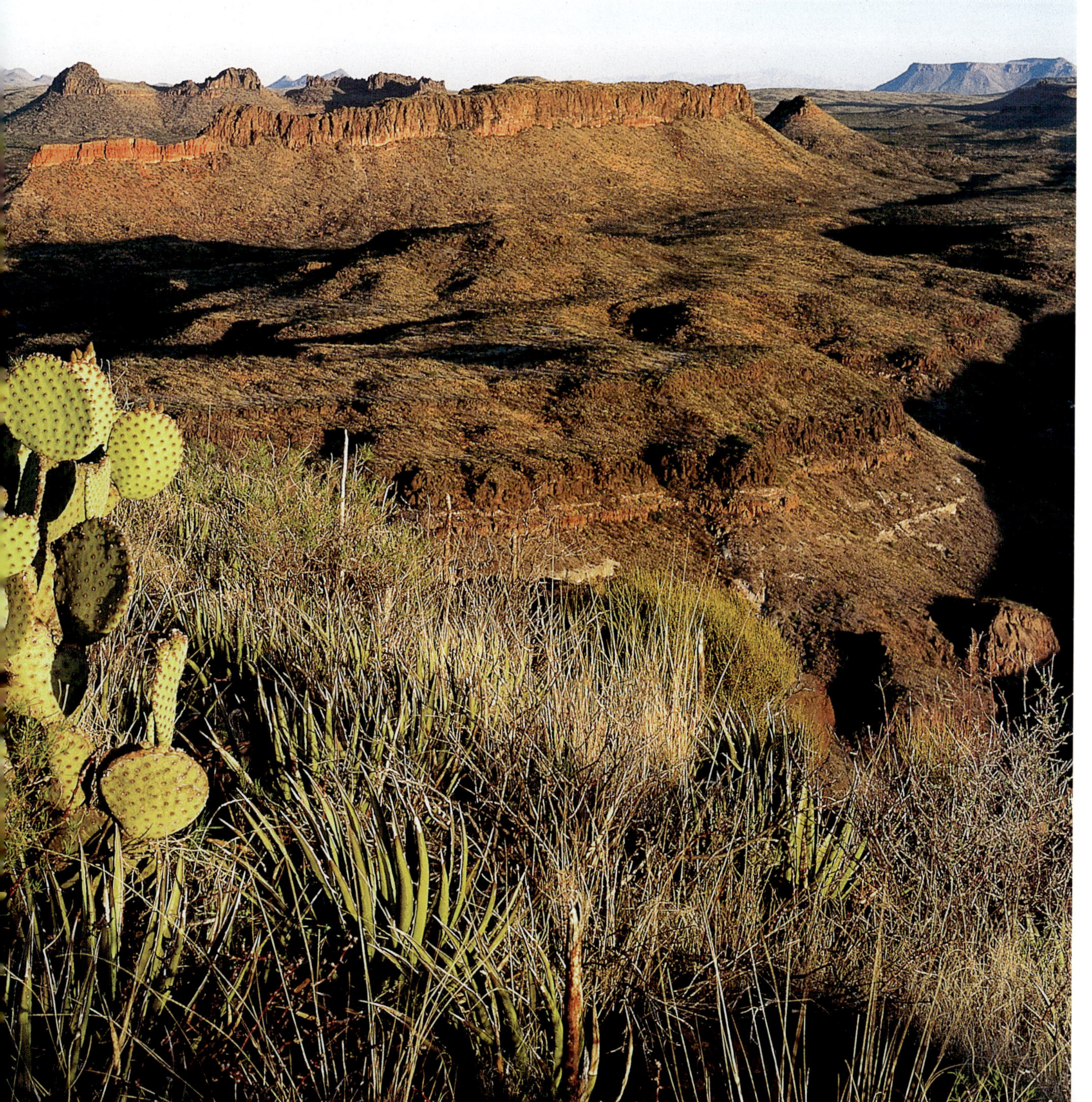

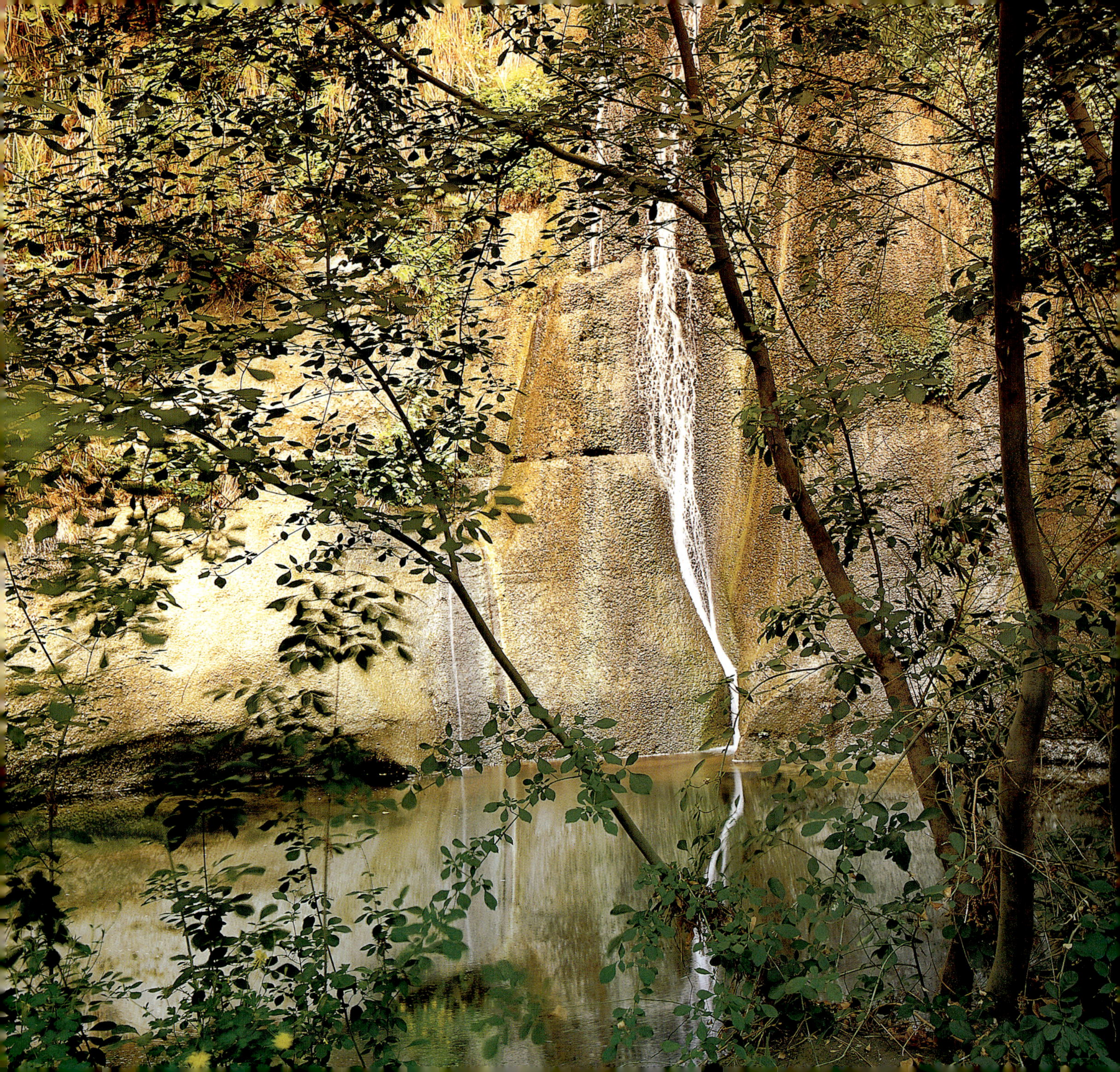

Madrid Falls, afternoon

Southern edge of Big Bend Ranch, near Colorado Canyon, looking southeast, late evening

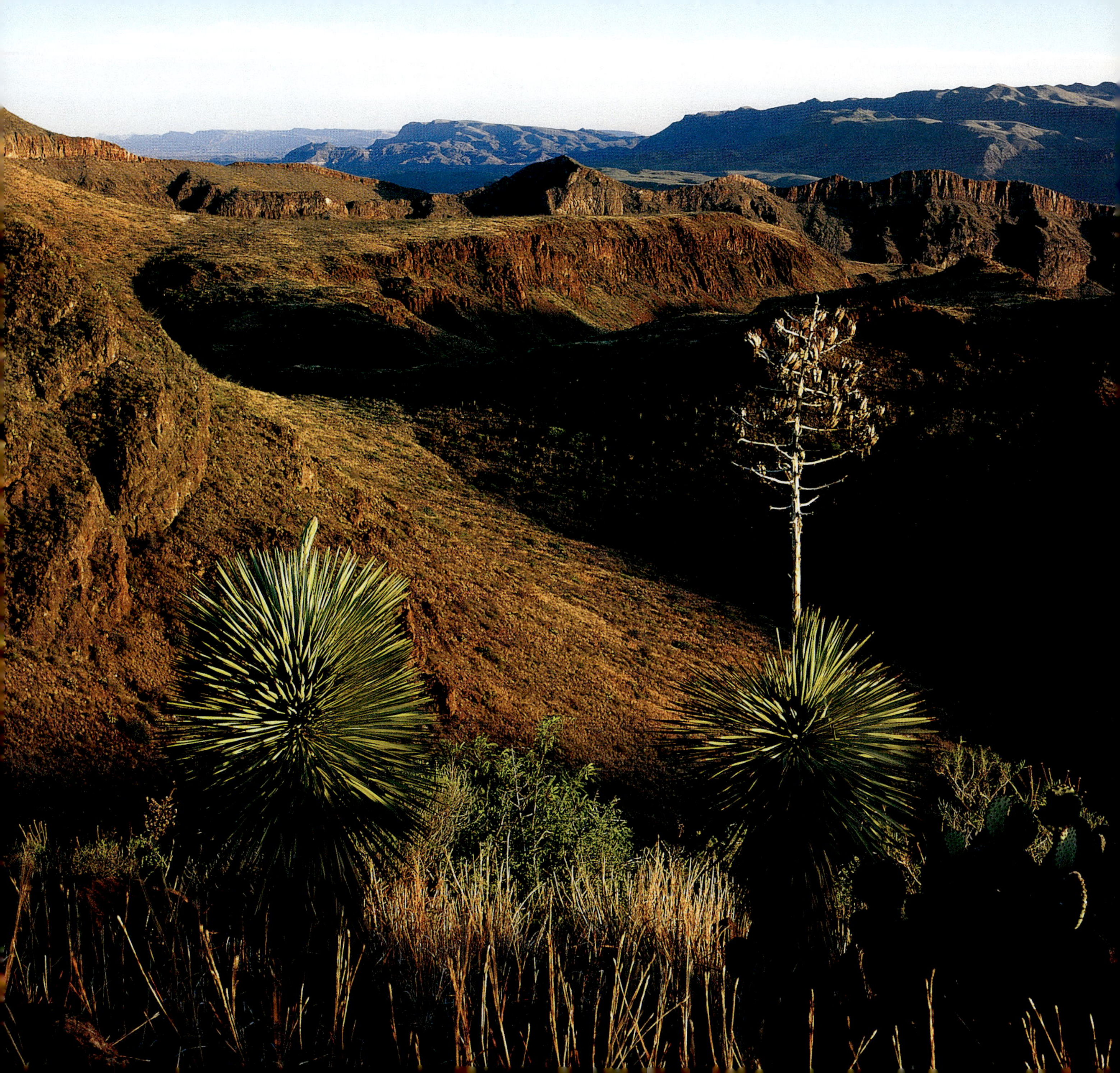

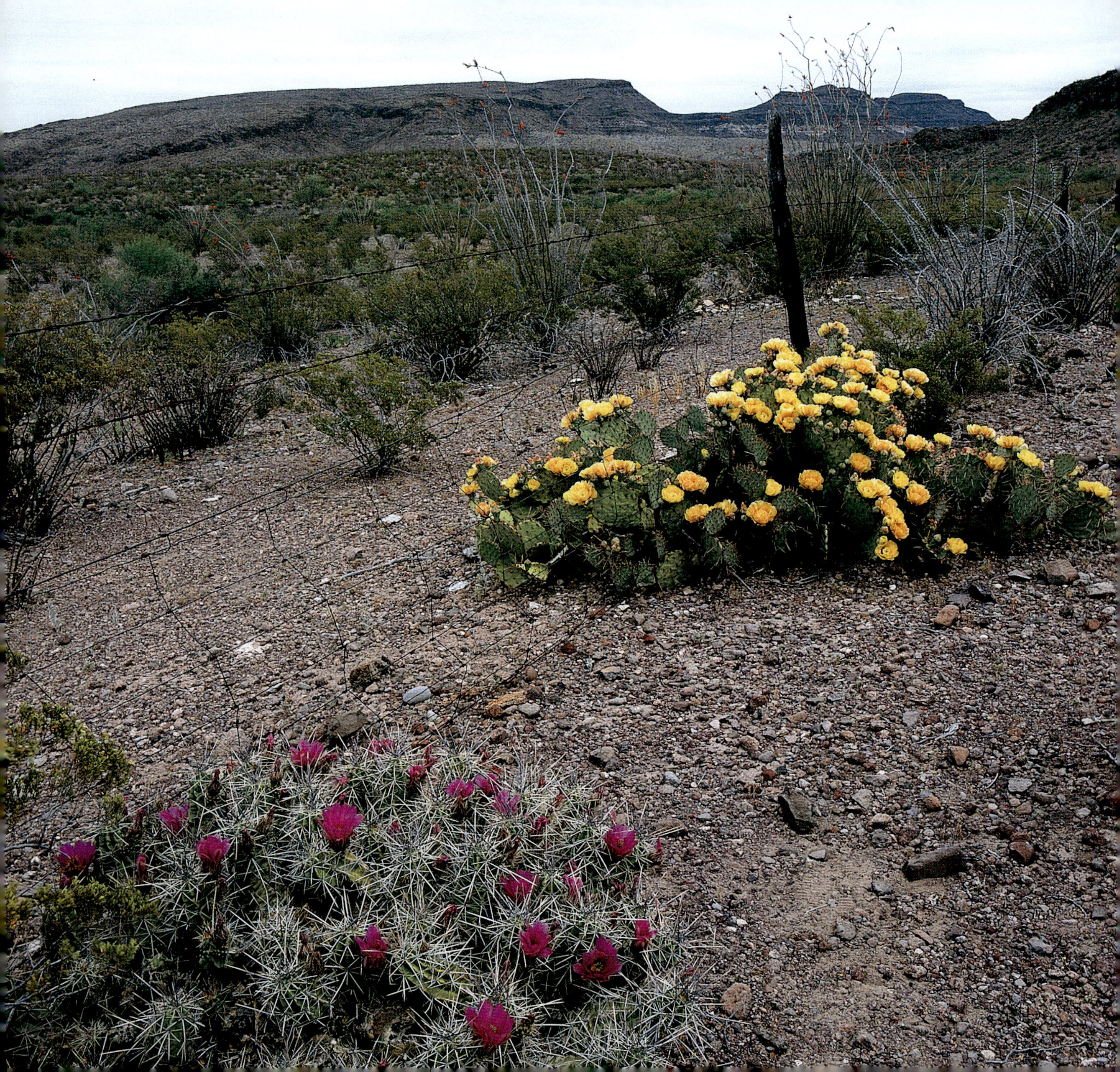

Claret cup and prickly pear blossoms, western edge Big Bend Ranch, looking northeast, midday

P H O T O G R A P H Y

Note: Unless otherwise noted, all photographs shot on Fujichrome Velvia film.

page ii: Hasselblad 500CM; Distagon 50MM f/4.0.
Figure 1: Hasselblad 500CM; Distagon 50MM f/4.0
Figure 2: Hasselblad 500CM; Zeiss Sonnar 150MM f/4.0
Figure 3: Hasselblad 500CM; Zeiss Sonnar 150MM f/4.0
Figure 4: Hasselblad 500CM; Zeiss Sonnar 150MM f/4.0
Figure 5: Hasselblad 500CM; Zeiss Sonnar 150MM f/4.0
Figure 6: Hasselblad 500CM; Zeiss Sonnar 150MM f/4.0
Figure 7: Hasselblad 500CM; Distagon 50MM f/4.0
Figure 8: Hasselblad 500CM; Zeiss Sonnar 150MM f/4.0
Figure 9: Hasselblad Bigon 38MM
Figure 10: Hasselblad 500CM; Zeiss Sonnar 150MM f/4.0
Figure 11: Hasselblad Bigon 38MM
Figure 12: Hasselblad 500CM; Zeiss Sonnar 150MM f/4.0
Figure 13: Hasselblad 500CM; Distagon 50MM f/4.0
Figure 14: Hasselblad 500CM; Distagon 50MM f/4.0
Figure 15: Hasselblad 500CM; Zeiss Planar 80MM f/2.8
Figure 16: Hasselblad 500CM; Zeiss Planar 80MM f/2.8
Figure 17: Hasselblad 500CM; Zeiss Planar 80MM f/2.8
Figure 18: Canon F1; Canon 20–35MM f/3.5
Figure 19: Canon EOS-1N; Canon 24MM Tilt-Shift
Figure 20: Canon EOS-1N; Canon 70–200MM Tilt-Shift
Figure 21: Canon F1N; 80–200MM f/4.0
Figure 22: Canon EOS-1N; Tilt-Shift f/3.5
Figure 23: Canon EOS-1N; Tilt-Shift f/3.5
Figure 24: Canon F1N; Canon 20–35MM f/3.5
Figure 25: Hasselblad Flexbody; Zeiss Sonnar 150 f/4.0
Figure 26: Hasselblad 500CM; Distagon 50MM f/4.0
Figure 27: Canon F1N; Canon 20–35MM f/3.5
Figure 28: Canon F1N; Canon 20–35MM f/3.5
Figure 29: Canon F1N; 80–200MM f/4.0
Figure 30: Canon F1N; 80–200MM f/4.0
Figure 31: Canon F1N; 80–200MM f/4.0
Figure 32: Canon F1N; Canon 20MM f/2.8; Kodachrome 64
Figure 33: Canon F1N; Canon 20–35MM f/3.5
Figure 34: Canon F1N; Canon 20–35MM f/3.5
Figure 35: Canon F1N; Canon 20–35MM f/3.5
Figure 36: Hasselblad 500CM; Zeiss Sonnar 150MM f/4.0
Figure 37: Hasselblad Flexbody; Zeiss Sonnar 150MM f/4.0
Figure 38: Hasselblad 500CM; Distagon 50MM f/4.0
Figure 39: Hasselblad 500CM; Zeiss Sonnar 150MM f/4.0
Figure 40: Hasselblad 500CM; Zeiss Sonnar 150MM f/4.0
Figure 41: Hasselblad 500CM; Distagon 50MM f/4.0
Figure 42: Hasselblad 500CM; Distagon 50MM f/4.0
Figure 43: Hasselblad 500CM; Zeiss Sonnar 150MM f/4.0
Figure 44: Hasselblad 500CM; Zeiss Planar 80MM f/2.8
Figure 45: Hasselblad 501CM; Distagon 50MM f/4.0
Figure 46: Hasselblad 501CM; Distagon 50MM f/4.0
Figure 47: Hasselblad 500CM; Distagon 50MM f/4.0
Figure 48: Hasselblad 500CM; Distagon 50MM f/4.0
Figure 49: Hasselblad 500CM; Planar 80MM f/2.8
Figure 50: Hasselblad 500CM; Distagon 50MM f/4.0
Figure 51: Hasselblad 501CM; Distagon 80MM f/4.0
Figure 52: Hasselblad 500CM; Planar 80MM f/2.8
Figure 53: Hasselblad Flexbody; Zeiss Sonnar 150MM f/4.0